AN ANXIOUS DEMOCRACY

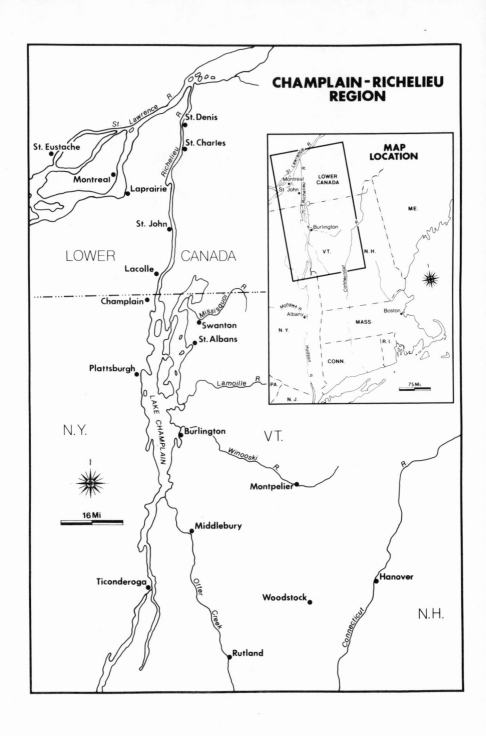

CHAMPLAIN-RICHELIEU REGION

AN ANXIOUS DEMOCRACY

Aspects of the 1830s

John J. Duffy and H. Nicholas Muller, III

CONTRIBUTIONS IN AMERICAN STUDIES,
NUMBER 58

GREENWOOD PRESS
Westport, Connecticut • London, England

Library of Congress Cataloging in Publication Data

Duffy, John J.
  An anxious democracy.

  (Contributions in American studies, ISSN 0084-9227; no. 58)
  Bibliography: p.
  Includes index.
    1. Vermont--History--Addresses, essays, lectures.
  2. Vermont--Social conditions--Addresses, essays, lec-
  tures. I. Muller, H. N. II. Title. III. Series.
  F49.5.D83   974.3'03   81-6387
  ISBN 0-313-22727-6 (lib. bdg.)   AACR2

Library of Congress Catalog Card Number: 81-6387
ISBN: 0-313-22727-6
ISSN: 0084-9227

First published in 1982

Greenwood Press
A division of Congressional Information Service, Inc.
88 Post Road West, Westport, Connecticut 06881

Printed in the United States of America

10 9 8 7 6 5 4 3 2 1

"There's much," he says, "about Vermont
For history and song,
Much to be written yet, and more
That has been written wrong. . . ."

Charles G. Eastman, "My Uncle Jerry," in
Poets and Poetry of Vermont, ed. by Abby Hemenway
(Rutland, Vermont, 1858).

CONTENTS

Illustrations   ix

Acknowledgments   xi

Abbreviations   xiii

Chapter One: Kicking Up a Cursed Dust   3

Chapter Two: An Aesculapius of the Soul   17

Chapter Three: Les Frères Chasseurs: A Vermont Tale   43

Chapter Four: The Great Wolf Hunt   57

Chapter Five: Civil Rebellion and the Nature of Man   87

Chapter Six: Vermonters Heroic and Otherwise   103

Chapter Seven: Phaedon or Bowditch   127

Chapter Eight: Nature's Roman Scourged   143

Sources   153

Index   165

ILLUSTRATIONS

Champlain-Richelieu Region   *frontispiece*

1. George Perkins Marsh, circa 1840, daguerreotype   78

2. James Marsh, circa 1835, oil portrait   79

3. Louis Joseph Papineau, circa 1830, lithograph by
   R. A. Sproule   80

4. Alonzo Jackman, circa 1860, photograph   81

5. Silas Jenison, circa 1840, steel engraving   82

6. "Old White Church," First Congregational
   Society, Burlington, Vermont   83

7. George Wyllys Benedict, circa 1850, daguerreotype   84

8. Joseph Torrey, circa 1860, photograph   85

9. Wolfred Nelson, circa 1850, sketch by
   Jean-Joseph Girouard   86

ACKNOWLEDGMENTS

We are deeply indebted to the studies of many scholars who
have preceded us in pursuit of the meanings of specific aspects
of events in both Vermont and the nation in the 1830s. The
size of our debt is immediately evident in the citations of works
by other writers on these topics. Our general synthesis of earlier
studies and our own investigations, however, as attempted here
invite testing and revision, both of which we encourage and seek.

Chapter Two first appeared in *Vermont History*, 46 (1978),
5-20, as "Jedidiah Burchard and Vermont's 'New Measure'
Revivals." Chapter Four was published in the *Journal of American
Studies*, 8 (1974), 153-69, as "The Great Wolf Hunt: The
Popular Response in Vermont to the *Patriotes* Uprising of 1837."

We are grateful for permission to use and publish materials
from the photographic and manuscript collections of Dartmouth
College, the University of Vermont, the Vermont Historical
Society, the Library of Congress, and the Public Archives of
Canada.

For their suggestions and criticisms we thank Professor Robert
Walker of George Washington University; Dr. James Sabin of
Greenwood Press; T. D. Seymour Bassett, former archivist of the
University of Vermont; David Blow; and members of the various

audiences who have heard and commented on sections of this study which were read to them at the Shelburne Museum Summer Lectures, the Vermont Academy of Arts and Sciences, the Vermont Studies Seminar of Johnson State College, and the sesquicentennial celebration of James Marsh's publication of Samuel Taylor Coleridge's *Aids to Reflection* (1829) sponsored by the Vermont Seminars of the University of Vermont.

A sabbatical leave from Johnson State College for John Duffy allowed time to conclude this study. Thus both of us are grateful to former President Edward Elmendorf for that grant. The University of Vermont provided valuable secretarial and research assistance to H. Nicholas Muller in the early stages of this study. For typing the final manuscript we thank Susan Mann of Johnson State College.

While writing this book during our respective tenures as administrators at Johnson State College, the University of Vermont, and Colby-Sawyer College, we might have occasionally caused some students or faculty to feel that their special needs or interests were only cursorily attended to as we progressed in this study. But any dean or department chairperson who has ever tried to carry out administrative duties, teach, research, and write will understand how much we appreciate the encouragement of the many students and faculty who urged our perseverance in this project. We apologize to those we might have failed to serve adequately and hope they will profit from this book.

ABBREVIATIONS

The following abbreviations are used for frequent citations or references:

UVM   University of Vermont

VHS   Vermont Historical Society

PAC   Public Archives of Canada

CAD   John Duffy, ed., *Coleridge's American Disciples: Selected Correspondence of James March* (Amherst, 1973).

JMC   Photocopy collection of James March's correspondence and other papers in the Bailey-Howe Library, UVM.

BV   Henry Crocker, *History of the Baptists in Vermont* (Bellows Falls, Vt., 1913).

AN ANXIOUS DEMOCRACY

CHAPTER ONE

KICKING UP A CURSED DUST

Violent social disruptions are rooted in both the psychology of the participants and their socioeconomic situation. Such disruptions also depend on shared cultural assumptions about the nature of power and the state and the relations of the individual and the group to them. In the 1830s, the numbers and types of social disruption in America and the unusual amount of violence they engendered—mob riots, lynchings, vigilante actions—suggest very deep roots and widely held assumptions and attitudes about the relation of the individual to society and its restraints.[1] A Baltimore newspaper noted in 1835 that only a cause "general in its operation" could explain the outbursts of social violence seen so frequently during that decade.[2]

Mass movements threatening violence or actual mob riots in eighteenth-century America carried a degree of official recognition as long as they did not attack the established political order. Colonial authorities thus continued the English tradition of allowing only minor influence on the government by the lower classes, while using these outbursts in the provincial governments' own assertions of local interests against the authority of the Crown.[3] But American independence and a broadened suffrage revoked the earlier sanctions for riot and similar social disruptions. Royall

Tyler's play *The Contrast* (1787) documents these changed attitudes toward violent rebellions. Tyler's hero, the naturally aristocratic Colonel Manly, persuades Jonathan, an ill-educated Yankee democrat, to desert Shays's Rebellion by reminding him that it "was a burning shame for the true blue Bunker Hill sons of liberty, who had fought Governor Hutchinson, Lord North, and the Devil to have any hand in kicking up a cursed dust against the government which we had, every mother's son of us, a hand in making."[4] Constituted authorities firmly crushed Shays's, Fries's, and the Whiskey Rebellions; and the earlier social or political purposes sanctioning unruly crowds or mobs were largely disallowed by 1800.

At the turn of the century and on into the period of the Embargo Act, when harsh feelings and barbed verbal attacks against Jefferson and the national government multiplied, mass gatherings with violent outcomes were seldom seen in America. After the War of 1812 and through the Era of Good Feelings, religious revivals, rather than violent mobs, became the most common group events.[5] But, while the revivals of the 1820s worked into another Great Awakening, in the last years of that decade and on into the 1830s group violence returned to prominence in American life. Between 1828 and 1835, at least seventy-three riots occurred, causing the Philadelphia *National Gazette* to state in 1835 that a "horrible fact is staring us in the face, that whenever the fury or cupidity of the mob is excited, they can gratify their lawless appetites almost with impunity; and it is wonderful . . . to behold the degree of supineness that exists."[6]

Indeed, during the mid-1830s, many Americans had a strong sense of social disintegration as groups frequently gathered for violent purposes. Yet peaceful intervals quickly followed the social disruptions and critical responses to the social disturbances became less fearful, soon becoming even formulaic as the decade wore on. Just as the religious revivals of the 1820s and 1830s had grown to resemble the widely spread religious movement of the 1750s known as the Great Awakening, violent social disturbances by 1835 also regained a position in American life which, unlike Shays's and Fries's eruptions, became accepted and, in some cases, approved, or at least silently acquiesced in, by the authorities.[7]

Tacit approval and, in some cases, quiet cooperation with riots, lynchings, or vigilante groups emerged because, in the words of Francis Grund in 1837, lynch law and riot are "not properly speaking an opposition to the established laws of the country. . . , but rather . . . a supplement to them."[8] Other defenders of mob riots or spokesmen for growing mass movements called such activities socially acceptable enforcements of justice that normal legal processes could not handle. Those who justified vigilance committees often invoked the Spirit of '76, claiming that American society from its very founding allowed popular, group actions to correct moral and social faults. The earlier, prerevolutionary justification for riotous social behavior did not return in the 1830s in its old form; it emerged, instead, as a basic tenet of American political independence, which came to maturity with the Age of Jackson's claims for the sovereignty of the individual, and encouraged men to gather in extraordinary groups with extra-legal intentions.

With a certain irony individual claims to sovereignty in turn made it difficult to oppose group assertions of the democratic right to redress real or perceived grievances. By emphasizing the role of the individual, the ideology and emotions during the 1830s both encouraged social disturbances and simultaneously discouraged efforts of the state to oppose them. As one defender of vigilante actions pointed out, "in America the individual is all and society nothing; . . . all aspects of the law are subordinated to individual right, which is the basis and essence of the republic."[9] Eugene Dumez's defense of vigilante actions goes but a short step beyond Emerson's "Trust thyself. Every heart vibrates to that iron string."[10] And so, too, James Fenimore Cooper's Natty Bumpo, like an Emersonian "representative man," would stand in sharp, dignified contrast to his fellow countrymen who could legally slaughter the annual flights of passenger pigeons or heedlessly fell noble maple trees for firewood, while Natty suffered prosecution for shooting a deer out of season.[11] Natty, like later American heroes from Huck Finn to Sam Spade,

lived by an individual code which did not threaten society
and instead served as a beacon for better social direction. As
de Tocqueville observed, many Americans believed that a "more
perfect union" was possible through "self interest rightly understood."[12]

In Vermont, socially disturbing mass movements, including
both threatened and real acts of violence, also rose to prominence during the 1830s. Unlike a mammoth but peaceful gathering of ten thousand spectators in 1809 at Burlington, many of
them fiercely anti-Jeffersonian, who came to witness the hang-
ing of an Embargo-breaking smuggler for the murder of Federal
revenue officers,[13] mass meetings throughout northern and
central Vermont during 1837-38 in support of the Canadian
patriote uprising threatened violence and indeed sent men to
take up arms and carry out their threats with resulting loss of
life.

The frenzied, sometimes violent group responses in Vermont
to the Canadian Rebellions of 1837-38 had been preceded by
fiery religious revivals which swept the state in 1835-36 in at
once a reflection of and a localized facet of the larger national revival movement. With the rest of the nation, and throughout
Vermont's various religious sects, including its small Catholic
population, the state experienced its portion of the Second Great
Awakening throughout the turbulent decade of the 1830s. Some
of the most dramatic events in Vermont's version of the Awakening came with Jedidiah Burchard and his New Measure revivals
which he conducted mostly in Vermont's Congregational churches. As a group event or moment of collective action, Vermonters' responses to and participation in Burchard's revivals as well
as the later mass meetings held to raise funds and gather weapons
in support of the Canadian *patriotes* involved all parts of the community. On the hill in Burlington in the cluster of buildings
around the shaggy college green overlooking the long waters of
Lake Champlain and the distant Adirondack Mountains, the
faculty of the University of Vermont could not remain aloof.
Their conscious intellectual pronouncements employed the
tempered language of abstraction and attempted appropriate

distance. But they could not avoid the raucous arguments at the foot of the hill where merchants, lawyers, ministers, editors, civil servants, judges, teamsters, laborers, factory hands, farmers, and students took sides. At one point a prominent merchant, angered by the conservative activities of the university faculty, threatened to cut off vital financial support from the community. The threat brought little apparent response, and two years later these same professors led the movement to petition the governor of Vermont to enforce neutrality during the aftermath of the *patriote* uprising.

The measured and analytical response of the scholar and the emotional outburst of the untrained both provide important clues to the psychology and situations of the participants and the assumptions and attitudes they held about themselves as individuals and groups. The academics had emerged from a set of conditions and experiences as had their fellow citizens down the hill or in the other Vermont communities wracked by the Burchard revivals and aroused by the rebellion in Lower Canada. The forces, the pushes and pulls, the tugs and spasms by which a society evolves, boiled to the surface during these two events which took place mostly in the northwestern part of Vermont during the 1830s. In some respects special to the time and place, these episodes were also general to the American experience of that decade. In the complex and interactive dynamics of social change in an open society a nation may take its cues from local events. At the same time the local events may confirm wider trends. The faculty of the University of Vermont, well versed in leading national and, indeed, broad transatlantic currents could not determine policy for an unreceptive public, though they could and did affect the course of public affairs. The public, for its part, as measured, for example, in mass meetings and other expressions of its view, also could not control policy, though the nation's capitol and other distant parts heard and responded to their clamor. While in their specific characteristics these disturbances involved only some Americans (frequently only Vermonters in response to either the Canadian Rebellions or the appearance in 1835 of an

enthusiastic religious revivalist in their midst), in their broader
characteristics these events seemed symptomatic of and, indeed,
probably mirrored the general condition of a people attempting
to define and direct themselves as a nation in especially stress-
ful times. Those stresses had their larger national expressions in
the continuing struggle to find adequate justifications for a specifically American way of seeing the world and defining one's place
in it. A review of the general national search for an ideology that
would justify the American experience thus becomes important
for understanding the relationship of special and apparently local
events to the general national experience. Satisfactory hypotheses
to provide an understanding or an adequate explanation of the
national experience, in turn, may require a thorough investigation of local events.

"Local history," declared Pierre Goubert, the dean of a new
school of French local historians, "has risen again and acquired
new meaning; indeed," he continued, "some even maintain that
only local history can be true and sound." The careful "practice
of local history and the multiplication of monographs on specific
regions" can provide the material from which a broad understanding of national affairs emerges, and as Goubert observed, it "may
serve to destroy many of the general conceptions that once seemed
so strong and were embodied in so many books, papers, and lectures."[14] Events in Vermont in the 1830s, then, when carefully
explored, can prove important to the delineation of the national
experience, but first the local scene demands description before
the development of "secure new generalizations to replace the discarded ones."[15] Even the intuitive genius of the historian who
can postulate a broad national hypothesis must wait for the work
of others to confirm its value.

"There's much," Charles G. Eastman's bent but unbending
Uncle Jerry said at the middle of the nineteenth century, "about
Vermont / For history and song, / Much to be written yet, and
more / That has been written wrong. . . ." Eastman, whom a
group of orthodox ministers had dispatched in 1835 to record
the errors of the revivalist Jedidiah Burchard, sensed that despite
the repeated chronicles of the pantheon of Vermont heroes, of

Ethan Allen, Seth Warner, Thomas Chittenden, and other Green
Mountain notables, "of even more important men / No record
has been made."[16] Uncle Jerry held his neighbors in higher
esteem than the enshrined for whom he harbored faint suspicions and not too well disguised contempt. He understood that
"good local history" can bring "a closer understanding of how
the common man reacted" and that it can treat "the history of
a whole society, not only the happy few who governed it, [or]
who judged it."[17]

Historians have begun to pay heed to Uncle Jerry's admoni-
tion. Vermont historians have discovered a century later that
neither the Allen version of Vermont history nor the work
that conceives of that history as an expanded edition of Allen's
biography provide an adequate account of Vermont's past.[18]
Yet the tyranny of the Allens over Vermont history stubbornly
persists, resting now on a foundation of a body of secondary
literature which has become the point of departure or the con-
textual framework for subsequent works.

The weakness in Vermont historiography, or in that of other
areas, engenders problems in the hypotheses and generalizations
which describe national history. The "building block" concept
construes local history as the essential building material in the
construction of a broad national history. Flaws in local history
threaten to become structural problems for the edifices built on
them. The theory of the building block conceives of writing
history as a deductive process building step by step, each element
resting on the preceding one. The quality of the whole rarely
achieves a quality greater than its constituent parts.

Historians, not unlike builders, usually begin with a plan.
The plan defines the evidence, the building materials they employ. The deductive process of the building block approach must
have a starting point (Genesis will not do), and as with builders
and architects, that point derives from a conception of the fin-
ished project. The historian curious about the Vermont response
to the *patriote* uprising will look for historical clues which describe and explain the events. The historian who asks questions
about the economic causes of the uprising or who conceives of

economic forces as central to the explanation of human en-
deavors will probably locate clues to economic forces which
define the Vermont response to the uprising.

The historian observes an event or phenomenon and then seeks
to explain it. In this manner historical questions, as all questions,
frequently dictate historical answers. First, the questions posed
limit the avenues of inquiry. The historian can rarely, if ever,
consider every shred of available information. The questions
help define what evidence is pertinent, a determination which
limits the evidence employed to a hypothesis. The larger the topic, the wider the inquiry, the smaller the portion of total available evidence the historian usually manages to consider. More
limited topics tend to allow a greater degree of consideration
of a body of evidence. In this way local history has a methodo-
logical advantage.

Answers, conversely, may dictate historical questions. Historians usually pose questions because of the fact of the answer.
The fact of the Vermont response to the *patriotes* invites questions about its causes. To inquire about the economic or social
origins invites an answer which defines that agitation in social or
economic terms. In this manner generalizations dangerously precede the collection of evidence and frequently limit that collection to items relevant to, if not supportive of, the hypothesis.
The broader the scope of the issue, the greater the possibility that
generalizations will precede the collection and analysis of evidence and the less the chances of bringing to bear all of the pertinent evidence. Of course, sound evidence properly employed
will modify the original hypothesis and, perhaps, even destroy
it, as it will also lead logically to sound generalizations. Incorrect
evidence, such as a weak or inaccurate local history, will weaken
the hypothesis and generalizations used to explain larger events.
Historians of national events, for example, by using unsound
materials to erect or to confirm their hypotheses, become hos-
tage to local history.

The view of the American response to the Canadian Rebellions of 1837-38 as the manifestation of the annexationist impulse, the organic sense of mission to spread democracy, or the

release of pent-up frustration created by the Panic of '37; or
the view of Jedidiah Burchard's revivals as the direct continua-
tion of the evangelical heat of the burnt-over district all con-
tain a measure of validity. But these interpretations do not
adequately explain these events in Vermont; and, thus, they
fail to serve as a sufficient explanation for these events at the
national level. A serious understanding of the response in Vermont to the *patriote* uprising offers a sound block in the foundation of a national treatment and suggestions for useful questions
to pose elsewhere.

Limits placed on a topic do not necessarily reduce its value.
Local history demands synthesis; it is not parochial in conception. Good local history transcends the self-limiting concept
of the case study, and local historians must remain wary of the
seductive and often limited construction of the case study, the
technical jargon which some scholars employ to lend respectability to their excursions into local events. The preface or conclusion of most case studies contains the accurate, modest, and
often ingenuous disclaimer that its conclusions should not be
transferred or extrapolated, thus paying homage to the reasonable assumption that, with infrequent exception, no two sets of
conditions are identical. In the first place the definition of well-
conceived history is not a function of geographic area, political
level, or other factors used to define "local." Good history is
just that, good history. The distribution of its publication does
not describe its quality, only its recognition. The most universal
aspects of human behavior do not conform to national or continental boundaries; they occur in a local setting and demand
(and in recent years have begun to receive) the full attention of
the best historical methodology. In the second place, an accurate
analysis of particular human behavior under one set of conditions will submit to an useful, if not direct, extrapolation. There
is nothing random about the fact that national movements,
trends, or ideas can almost always be detailed at the local level.
Perhaps it is tautological to suggest that national trends have
local expression, but the fact does raise important questions
of cultural diffusion and the dynamics of leadership and change

in America. A sound local history details the origins of trends
perceived as such on a larger stage, and it can suggest the reasons
for rejection or acceptance of once alien ideas.

History, viewed as an intellectual construction used as a convenient tool to aid in the analysis and explanation of human behavior, employs essentially similar methodology at all levels; its
scope differs largely in the limits suggested by events and arbitrari-
ly imposed by historians. The Age of Jackson never existed; it
developed in the minds of the historians as a convenient means
to understand and describe a set of phenomena and events related
through time and chronology, through similarity in form and participants, and through the historians' attempt to ascribe clear
cause and effect to the murky affairs of past generations. The
concept of the Age of Jackson is useful to help select and arrange
evidence through a set of arbitrary limits. Choosing other arbitrary
limits, confining an investigation to a geographic area or locality,
the only operative definition of local history, does not diminish
the potential for historical validity. The only limiting aspect of
local history is the territorial definition, which is, of course,
similar to the definition of state, regional, national, or continental
history. The nature of the boundaries then, not the concept of
history, sets aside local history.

Yet local history has received the disdain of the professional
historians partly "because of their own conception of what they
chose to see as 'general' history. General history was political,
military, diplomatic, administrative. . . . Studying the state involved a study of statesmen, studying war permitted a study of
the military feats of generals . . ." and so on.[19] Another part of
a lingering disdain for local history came about because of the
antiquarian nature of some local history. Blinders firmly in place,
the local historian sometimes worked with a devotion motivated
by personal or sentimental ties to the subject or place. These efforts only rarely exhibited control of historical methodology,
the understanding of external events, or the willingness to syn-
thesize. Like the results of family genealogists, not surprisingly,
local history has sometimes followed an arrangement of detail
on a town, village, or county basis which resembles a genea-

logical treatment. The value of these efforts should not be over-looked, nor should they be confused with good history.

Good local history matches good national history in most aspects, and their combination prevents the spread of "a gloss of hazy generalities over clear specifics."[20] Broad national treatments without the benefit of a well-developed local or regional historiography must generalize from evidence weakened by the limits of time or capacity. Even the historical accounts of a state, as Uncle Jerry warned, will suffer if they concentrate on the luminaries and ignore the common people.

This study, then, begins with a specific consideration of a set of events which occurred in northwestern Vermont first in 1835 and then the winter of 1837-38; it then goes on to consider a larger framework of ideas in which the behavior of Vermonters in their place and time can be understood. The disparate responses in Vermont to the Canadian Rebellions or Jedidiah Burchard's New Measure revivals emerge as pointed examples of the continuing efforts in the nation to live within the tensions of a growing democratic society and to carry on the task of formulating an American ideology that would help its citizens cope with the stresses such tensions induce. That national effort required theories of perception and expression that could comprehend and give intelligible voice to the full range of democratic experiences and values. And these attempts to cope with internal social stresses and formulate such theories engaged American energies during the entire antebellum period.

NOTES

1. *See* James F. Kirkham, Sheldon G. Levy, and William J. Crotty, *Assassination and Political Violence* (New York, 1970), 228-29.

2. *Baltimore Republican,* August 20, 1835.

3. Pauline Maier, "Popular Uprisings and Civil Authority in Eighteenth-Century America," *William and Mary Quarterly,* 27 (1970), 3-35; and Gordon Wood, "A Note on Mobs in the American Revolution," *William and Mary Quarterly,* 23 (1966), 635-42.

4. Royall Tyler, *The Contrast* (New York, 1970), 56.

5. Bernard Weisberger, *They Gathered at the River: The Story of*

the Great Revivalists and Their Impact Upon Religion in America (Chicago, 1966), chapters 1-4; and Donald G. Mathews, "The Second Great Awakening as an Organizing Process, 1780-1830," *American Quarterly*, 21 (1969), 22-43.

6. *Philadelphia National Gazette,* August 11, 1835.

7. Richard Maxwell Brown, "The American Vigilante Tradition," in Hugh Davis Graham and T. R. Gurr, eds., *Violence in America: A Documentary History* (New York, 1970), 181.

8. Francis Grund, *The Americans in Their Moral, Social and Political Relations* (Boston, 1837), 180.

9. Eugene Dumez, in Alexandre Barde, *Histoire des Comités de Vigilance aux Attakapas* (St. Jean-Baptiste, La., 1861), iv, quoted in David Grimsted, "Rioting in Its Jacksonian Setting," *American Historical Review,* 77 (1972), 364. Here and in our final chapter we are greatly indebted to Grimsted for his perceptive analysis of social disruptions in the 1830s.

10. Ralph Waldo Emerson, "Self Reliance," in *Complete Works* (Boston, 1895), I, 19. Quentin Anderson finds Emerson to be an important contributor to the American habit "of stretching the moral imperatives of individual conduct to cover the aims of the nation-state. . . . Emerson helped to make the overextension of the significance of individual claims seem a positive value before the middle of the last century . . . [by] advising his fellows to hitch their wagons to a star." This American peculiarity, for Anderson, indicates "the vacuum that exists in place of a communally shared sense of goal, or indeed of being." (*The Imperial Self: An Essay in American Literary and Cultural History* [New York, 1971], 18.)

11. James Fenimore Cooper, *The Pioneers* (New York, 1823).

12. Alexis de Tocqueville, *Democracy in America,* ed. by Philip Bradley (New York, 1957), II, 131.

13. On August 4, 1808, the smuggler crew of the cutter *Blacksnake* resisted revenue officers who surprised them as they prepared to take a load of potash down Lake Champlain into Canada. Captured and charged with killing three of the revenue men, the smugglers finally faced trial after repeated dismissals of potential jurymen, like Ethan Allen, Jr., who felt that the smugglers were innocent of any crime because their actions were anti-Embargo. Cyrus Dean was sentenced to be hanged for killing an officer, and his execution was carried out on Court House Square in Burlington on November 11, 1809. No riot or disturbance occurred. *See* John Duffy, ed., *Early Vermont Broadsides* (Hanover, N.H., 1975), 19; H. N. Muller, III, "Smuggling into Canada: How the Champlain Valley Defied Jefferson's Embargo," *Vermont History,* 38 (1970), 5-21; and *Vermont Centinel,* August 5, 10, and 12, 1808. Muller records the numerous town meetings held in Vermont, particularly in the Champlain Valley, during 1808 at which loud protests against the Embargo were voiced and in fact voted as resolutions. Mass violence, however, was rumored rather than

factual. Smuggling was too profitable an enterprise for both smugglers and revenue officers, who stored captured exports intended for Canada, to risk government suppression in response to massive violent resistance to the hated trade restriction with England and its colonies. Muller, "Smuggling," 14-16.

14. Pierre Goubert, "Local History," *Daedalus*, 100, No. 1 (Winter 1971), 113 and 119.

15. Bruce C. Daniels, *The Connecticut Town* (Middletown, Conn., 1979), 4.

16. Charles G. Eastman, "My Uncle Jerry," in Abby Maria Hemenway, ed., *Poets and Poetry of Vermont* (Rutland, 1858), 62-70.

17. Goubert, "Local History," 117.

18. *See* J. Kevin Graffagnino, "The Vermont 'Story': Continuity and Change in Vermont Historiography," *Vermont History*, 46 (1978), 77-99.

19. Goubert, "Local History," 115.

20. Daniels, *Connecticut Town*, 5.

CHAPTER TWO

AN AESCULAPIUS OF THE SOUL

Controversy and contradiction were endemic to the American scene in the 1830s, and foreign visitors to America noticed these symptoms and recorded them. The popular English novelist, Frederick Marryat, travelling in late 1837 from Canada into Vermont "through what were termed the *excited* districts" because of the *Patriote* rebellion in Canada, remarked on the hectic frenzy of the American people, who he found were easily excited "and when excited, they will hesitate at nothing. The coach (for it was the stage-coach although represented by an open sleigh), stopped at every town, large or small, everybody eager to tell and receive news [of the *patriotes*]. . . . [I] heard all the remarks made upon what I do really believe were the most absurd and extravagant lies which were put into newspapers, and circulated every where."

Soon after crossing the border Marryat fell in with the *patriote* leader Thomas Storrow Brown, whom the English novelist found remarkable only for "his very fine pair of mustachios." Marryat's

An earlier version of this chapter appeared as John J. Duffy and H. Nicholas Muller, III, "Jedidiah Burchard and Vermont's 'New Measure' Revivals: Social Adjustment and the Quest for Unity." Reprinted from the Winter, 1978, issue of *Vermont History*, courtesy of the Vermont Historical Society.

visit to Saint Albans, however, confirmed his original impressions
of Americans. Two of the three inns in Saint Albans were the
noisy resorts of philo*patriotes* "and in these, consequently, scenes
of great excitement took place."[1]

Other English travellers in the 1830s, such as the censorious
Mrs. Trollope, often remarked on the contradictions in America
that seemed to contrast life in the young country with the stability
and orderliness of their homeland.[2] But even though Mrs. Trollope
was inclined to put the worst interpretation on everything she saw—
"I do not like their principles, I do not like their manners, I do not
like their opinions"[3]—she still recorded the apparent contradictions in events and behavior characteristic of a people struggling
to define and assert their own collective identity and in various
ways exhibiting the anxieties and strains of that struggle.

Mrs. Trollope observed the excessive American concern with
sociosexual decorum and pointed directly to how affectations
had been substituted for traditionally developed modes of social
behavior in a time when appearances, or what many Americans
thought behavior ought to be, contradicted reality. In Cincinnati
a young German immigrant anxiously inquired of her how to
apologize to one of the city's leading families for mentioning the
word "corset" in the presence of ladies. At Philadelphia's Pennsylvania Academy, she also discovered, men and women never
entered or viewed together the gallery of antique nude statutes
exhibited there (p. 83). On the other hand, the emotional excesses
of a religious revival she attended demonstrated with unmistakably
sexual overtones the absence of restraint in socioreligious matters
when compared to the affected delicacies of sociosexual behavior.[4]

The archetypal revival scene she viewed in Ohio had become
such a persistent feature of the American landscape in the 1830s
that the era became known as the time of the Great Revival. Mrs.
Trollope was repelled, she would have her readers believe, by the
emotional outpourings of sexual guilt so apparent at an Ohio
camp meeting. Stoutly maintaining her solid English sense of
propriety for the entire two hours that she watched, she noticed
that "beautiful young females" predominated in the group of
penitents called forward from the huge crowd by the revivalists.

"The preacher moved about among them, at once exciting and soothing their agonies," as Mrs. Trollope witnessed the event in shocked, yet fascinated, amazement.

> I heard the muttered 'Sister! dear Sister!' I saw the insidious lips approach the cheeks of the unhappy girls; I heard the murmured confessions of the poor victims, and I watched their tormentors, breathing into their ears consolations that tinged the pale cheek with red. Had I been a man, I am sure I should have been guilty of some rash act of interference; nor do I believe that such a scene could have been acted in the presence of Englishmen without instant punishment being inflicted . . . to check so turbulent and so vicious a scene. [p. 127]

The revivalists separated a mass of nearly one hundred repentant sinners from the crowd into a "pen" in front of the stage. The sinners sprawled "on the ground in an indescribable confusion of heads and legs. . . . [in] incessant and violent motion" (p. 126). One "very pretty girl, who was kneeling in the attitude of Canova's Magdalene," cried out her repentance.

> Woe! woe to the backsliders! I hear it, hear it, Jesus! when I was fifteen my mother died, and I backslided! take me home to my mother, Jesus! take me home to her, for I am weary! Oh John Mitchel! John Mitchel!

"But I saw her," Mrs. Trollope finally noted, "ere I left the ground, with her hand fast locked and her head supported by a man who looked very much as Don Juan might, when sent back to earth as too bad for the region below" (p. 127).

Even allowing for Mrs. Trollope's biases, and none of the other English travellers in America achieved her level of acerbic Americaphobia, the report of the apparent contradictions between the fastidious concern with delicacies of speech and sexual matters that so disturbed the young German immigrant and the public confessions of sexual guilt at the camp meeting still ring true.

Although just as censorious as Mrs. Trollope in his reports on
the American scene, the English traveller Thomas Hamilton was
one of her few travelling contemporaries to recognize a point recently made by social scientists, "that in a newly settled country
the strong effect produced by these camp meetings and revivals
is on the whole beneficial . . . in such circumstances, the higher
principle of action, communicated by religion, is a new and additional security to society." For Hamilton, revivals helped to
organize society.[5] Modern scholars now realize that those revivals
of the early nineteenth century indeed played an important role
in the development of American society. As some recent studies
have shown, the revivals of the Second Great Awakening functioned as a social organizing process in American life from the
turn of the nineteenth century until as late as perhaps 1860.[6]

Tracing the origins of the Great Revival or Second Great Awakening back to the enthusiastic Baptist and Methodist missionaries
of Virginia and North Carolina in the 1770s, Donald Mathews,
for example, showed how the ubiquitous revival meeting turned
many people into participating members of society at large in an
age when church membership provided social as well as religious
standing. While both the First Awakening of the 1740s and 1750s
as well as the Second Awakening shared the tremendous resur-
gence of revivalistic religious experiences, the quantitative extension of church life by Methodists, Baptists, and in some cases
evangelical Presbyterians and Congregationalists, clearly distinguished the Second Awakening from its predecessor.[7] The
Tocquevillian truism found evangelical religion everywhere by
1835. Evangelicalism, apart from its theological aspects, constituted more than an isolated social phenomenon, but instead
exhibited all of the characteristics of a socially organizing process—
it had unity, organization, and movement. The Second Great
Awakening "in its social aspects was an organizing process that
helped to give meaning and direction to people suffering in
various degrees from the social strains of a nation on the move
into new political, economic, and geographical areas."[8]

As with the rest of the nation during the turbulent decade of
the 1830s, it was clear that vast changes had come to Vermont

and, particularly worrisome, that they showed every sign of permanency. Perhaps the War of 1812 had signalled a turning point in the small state's fortunes, at least in men's minds. Actually, the war with its economic dislocations, the severe epidemic of the mysterious and deadly "spotted fever" (cerebrospinal meningitis), and the isolation brought on by Federalist politics may only have punctuated changes already well under way. Before the unpopular war the burgeoning state had experienced the nation's fastest rate of population growth and exulted in the easy promise that most ventures would succeed, and many handsomely. Only a few short years later the boom psychology and its attendant sense of confidence in the future were badly shaken and in steady retreat.

As if preordained by some higher power, a series of natural disasters afflicted Vermont. In the terrible summer of 1816 frost and snow came every month, destroying several successive plantings and provoking a trickle of discouraged emigration that in a few years broadened into a rushing stream. By the 1830s Vermonters had wantonly cut off most of their rich heritage of timber and with the forest gone had begun to experience the harmful effects of "dry spells." Conversely, a series of disastrous storms and the resultant freshets washed out mill sites (two-thirds of the mills in Rutland and Windsor Counties in 1811),[9] carried away much of the rich alluvial soil of the intervales, destroyed bridges, barns, and crops, and drowned livestock. Then came a plague of grasshoppers, the wheat rust, and the distressing evidence of general soil exhaustion, and with all of them the yield of Vermont's fields rapidly declined. The canals that had promised a much needed outlet for Vermont's produce instead perversely became arteries for the migration of her sons and daughters stricken with the "Western craze" and for the introduction of competitive products from the new West. Even the game animals and fish that had once abounded in her forests and waters were all but extinct by the mid-1830s.[10]

The drastic change in the pace of life in Vermont was starkly apparent by the 1830s, and it was evident that serious adjustments would have to be realized, though there was little agreement as to the direction the adjustments should take. In 1820

liabilities exceeded assets, and ten years later the growth of population barely kept pace with the emigration. The newcomers
seldom resembled the familiar old Yankee stock. In 1832 the
threat of cholera posed a frightening menace and during the
next decade rude sheds dotted the Burlington waterfront housing
Irish immigrants waiting to die or be released to find meagre
sustenance in a hostile environment.[11] The old family farms
frequently gave way to sheep folds in a northern New England
version of the enclosures, and the shift away from labor-inten-
sive agriculture helped alter both the economic base and the
traditional pattern of landholding. In sheep-crazed Addison
County the woolly animals grazed 373 to the square mile.[12]
Anti-Jacksonian throughout the 1830s, Vermonters felt politically cut off and were quick to hold "King Andrew" and his political henchmen responsible for many of their economic woes,
especially after the Panic of 1837.

Such a setting, in which people had experienced a rapid and
sometimes violent reversal in their prospects for the future,
provided fertile ground for a lively, almost frenetic political
and social ferment. The voters turned to the Anti-Mason Party,
which held the governor's office from 1831 through 1836, and
provided all seven of the electoral ballots cast for the Anti-Mason
presidential candidate William Wirt in 1832. The state quickly
embraced, one on top of the other, most of the national movements and fads and even generated a number of its own. The
temperance crusade headed by the Vermont Temperance Society
after 1828 worked through its more than two hundred local clubs
to dry up the state by force of moral suasion. The temperance
activities had to compete for enthusiasm with the Working Men's
movement, prison reform, care for the unfortunate, education
reform, the abolition of imprisonment for debt, and the mount-
ing fury over slavery. William Lloyd Garrison published one of
his first antislavery blasts in Bennington in 1828 and helped
evoke the early rumblings of the issue that gripped the state for
three decades.

In 1837 when the *patriotes* of Lower Canada declared independence from Britain and started an optimistic but short-
lived rebellion, Vermonters eagerly embraced the cause. In their

noisy enthusiasm for the *patriotes,* as in their ardor for a host
of other movements that swept the state, Vermonters tried to
adjust to new circumstances and regain a nebulous but nonetheless important collective sense of common purpose.

In the forefront of the ferment in Vermont were the mil-
lennialists, visionaries, and evangelists who crisscrossed the
state with a variety of religious missions. In Putney John
Humphrey Noyes began his celebrated community based on
spiritual communism and the widening of sexual bonds, including the formula of male continence. Joseph Smith, the founder
of the Latter Day Saints, began his trek in Sharon; Swedenborgianism flourished in Cambridge in the Lamoille River valley; and
William Miller brought many adventist converts across the entire
state to his exuberant view of the Second Coming and the im-
minent end of the world.

Beginning during the War of 1812 but most strongly during
the 1830s, waves of revivalism rolled across the state engendering
profound mental and even physical upset. Thousands were pros-
trated with religious fervor. Few orthodox churches escaped the
disruption, and many were permanently split. The revivals continued unabated until 1840 and in many aspects paralleled the
more secular movements of the decade as Vermonters sought
to deal with their prevailing discontent.

Students of collective behavior point to the development
of social movements, revivals, for example, as the remedial
actions of groups of people to allay the strains of uncertainty
and confusion in changing times. The strain can often be ambiguous, the mysterious product of many tangled and complex
factors, which though sensed in perplexing, vague, and muddled
terms, present a very real threat to men's ambitions and to seem-
ingly stable social institutions. When, in a given situation, a threat
can be clearly perceived—George III's Hessians in the 1770s, Jefferson's Embargo later, or armed forces on the Canadian-United
States border during the Lower Canadian rebellion in 1837-38—
energies can be directed into battles, public meetings, and strongly worded resolutions of defense and mutual support. When its
origin proves nebulous, difficult to isolate and define, the menace
can be nonetheless real, and the society will eagerly seek outlets

which frequently assume a dynamic of their own. Throughout the 1830s the growing volume of social pressure generated a variety of mass movements; and when the religious revival that Charles Grandison Finney had fired into life nearly a decade earlier made its way through the Congregational and other churches of Vermont in 1835 and 1836, many habitually taciturn Yankees flocked to it with anxious zeal. At the same time the revival provoked a serious and lively public debate that measured the intensity of the issue and spoke directly to the immediate questions of the organization of societal relationships and the direction in which they should proceed.

The revival came first to the Connecticut River valley towns and swept westward across Vermont largely on the feverish efforts of an itinerant revivalist, the Reverend Jedidiah Burchard.[13] Once a haberdasher, travelling actor, and a circus rider, he had been converted by Finney in the early thirties at a revival in the Oneida region of New York's "Burnt-Over District." The "celebrated revival preacher" came into Vermont in 1835 and held a series of "protracted meetings" mostly in the Congregational churches of "Woodstock, Windsor, Weathersfield, Springfield, Cornish (Baptist Society), Claremont, Charlestown, Croyden, Lebanon, Hanover, Norwich, Montpelier, Rutland, Middlebury, Williston, Hinesburg, Royalton and Burlington."[14]

In this version of the Lord's battle "all the preaching and exhortation [were] to bring saints and sinners to feel that they must have all their hopes of good upon the [grace] of God and upon the Holy Spirit . . . [for] without his agency no permanent good could be done."[15] Burchard conducted revival meetings with the "new measure system" he had learned from Finney and had refined through his own practice. He reserved special pews or seats, called "anxious seats," in the front of the church for those who were especially concerned for their souls, and mass public prayers were elicited from the meeting for designated sinners in the town, often those who publicly opposed or resented Burchard. "Protracted meetings" usually lasted several weeks, such as the revival in Burlington in December 1835 which endured for twenty days with Burchard preaching at most of the public services in the afternoon and evening while "neighboring clergymen sustained chiefly the other parts of the labor."[16]

Burchard's own enormous talent for oratory was thoroughly exercised in arousing the congregation to a fever pitch of excitement and overwhelming expressions of emotion which convinced the congregation that they had been witnesses to conversions or had themselves been saved and thus become rightful members of a holy community. "In the transport of exhortation," one observer reported, the former circus performer "would leap from the pulpit and do acrobatic stunts in front of it and walk among the people on the tops of the backs of the square pews."[17]

Burchard drew large groups to the meetings he held in Vermont and claimed hundreds of successful conversions to Christ and new members for the church in each town he visited. The New Measures also attracted a wide cross section of the predominantly Protestant communities. In his revival in the First Congregational Church in Burlington, "the members of the church with few exceptions came into the work." During the twenty day meeting "there were about 200 cases of professed submission to Jesus Christ. Of these about one-third were male and female heads of families."[18] According to the account of an eager university student, "the converts . . . included men of all ages and ranks. The old and the young, the sick and the poor, the learned and the illiterate" shared in the experience. Among the young, five students from the University of Vermont (10 percent of the undergraduate enrollment) and several Sunday school boys gave "themselves to Christ."[19] The First Congregational Church counted 101 new members, 5 of whom "were received from other churches."[20] When Burchard journeyed out of Burlington, his "converts follow[ed] him about everywhere. Many of them went to Williston . . . and some . . . followed him to Hinesburg" where he brought "together all the country round."[21] Ministers of congregations that had experienced Burchard's spell testified to the strength of his evangelical persuasion. The minister of Woodstock stated that "he never had the least cause to regret that such a meeting was holden in his church."[22]

But not everyone in Woodstock shared the pastor's enthusiasm for Burchard, and at a town meeting the selectmen branded him "a public nuisance."[23] From the very start of his Vermont campaign, Burchard antagonized many citizens. Usually, though not always, the anti-Burchardites were led by "the soundest clergymen," who opposed the itinerant preacher on social as well as theological grounds.[24]

In February 1836, the Congregationalist ministers belonging to the Rutland Association met because "the system of meas[ures] . . . for exciting + promoting revivals of religion . . . in operation during the year past among the churches of Vermont was expected soon to be introduced within their own limits." Clearly threatened, these "ministers of the gospel and stewards of the household of God" resolved to a man to try to keep the revivals out of their churches. In their view the New Measure "system of operations . . . strongly tend to interfere with the responsibilities of the established clergy." The revivals stripped spiritual guidance from those "who by their office must be responsible," and forfeited it to "those who have never qualified themselves for the task, and who cannot be supposed to feel the same responsibility."[25]

Their objections, however, went beyond the immediate threat to their own status. They thought Burchard's movement endangered the very institution of the church by "compromising + exposing to dishonor the sound congregationalism of New England" itself. The Measures turned people from the true meaning of the church by introducing "an unsubdued spirit of levity + of bustling disorder." The revivalists were "not merely untasteful, but indecently low + personal . . . + [used] harsh unchristian language . . . wholly at variance with elevated christian feeling." They declared that "such things cannot fail to expose to profane scoffing, that religion, which they so grievously misrepresent." The revivals, concluded these self-proclaimed "authorized spiritual guides" of the Rutland Association, "must tend very essentially + very injuriously to alter the character of the congregational churches."[26]

Except at Williston and Middlebury, where local ministers warmly received Burchard and supported his revivals, especially Middlebury where the president of Middlebury College, Joshua Bates, stood foursquare behind Burchard, town fathers or members of the professional classes generally shunned the New Measures.[27] President Bates's spirited stance on the revival cost him support among his faculty, who in large part joined their counterparts at the University of Vermont in outspoken criticism of "Burchardism."[28] Along with college faculty and the "powerful" of the community, opposition came from the "Episcopals and Unitarians," who direly predicted that the movement would "give triumph to the cause of infidelity and everything that is bad."[29] For their role in opposing Burchard, University of Vermont's President John Wheeler and Professor James Marsh, the former president and noted Coleridge scholar, "were accused of truckling to the Unitarians, [or] of being Unitarians at least."[30] Because of his publications alluding to the "highly pernicious" results of Burchard's measures in New York, Bishop John Henry Hopkins of the Episcopal Diocese of Vermont brought both himself and his flock into "bad odour with the *majority*."[31]

Burchard's Burlington converts were extremely unhappy with the Rutland Association's stance on the revival and feared that their own Chittenden County group might adopt it also. They issued a brief rebuttal of the Rutland report in defense of the New Measures. While the Rutland divines "more than insinuate that there [sic] effects are fanatical + divisive," the Burlington men professed to "believe + firmly believe" the movement to be wrought by the "truth + spirit of God." There was little room for compromise between two groups who each opposed the other in the firm belief that they knew the will of God.[32]

The revival sharply divided both churches and communities, leaving little opportunity for neutrality. While its enthusiastic adherents publicly committed their souls, the detractors believed that the New Measures rendered "the churches in a dissipated state of mind, which unfits them for all common duties and creates a disrelish for the daily routine of life."[33] Good Christians took firm stands on either side of the issue and quickly discarded the standard virtues of tolerance and forbearance. "We are almost at loggerheads here about what is called 'Burchardism,'" wrote University of Vermont Professor G. W. Benedict. "Some of our friends," he continued, "who are carried away with Mr. Burchard's quackery think it next to a mortal sin that we do not think him as great an Aesculapius of souls as they do especially that we should have the boldness to say so frankly."[34] Yet even Burchard's admirers admitted that "in the heat of his zeal he says some things which he had better not say."[35]

When his opponents, possibly including leaders of the University of Vermont faculty, in an appeal to public common sense took steps to publish his most outrageously unsound theological statements, the resultant furor endangered the very existence of the university. During the protracted meetings at Woodstock, Burchard's antagonists had dispatched a reporter to the church where he preached in order to take notes from the sermons and other proceedings. Russell Streeter gathered together the notes and printed the most flamboyant and offensive parts along with the selectmen's resolution condemning the itinerant preacher.[36] When Burchard came to Burlington, Chauncey Goodrich, publisher and bookseller as well as brother-in-law to Professor Marsh, hired two undergraduates, Charles G. Eastman and B. J. Tenney, to attend the concurrent meetings in Burlington and nearby Williston in order to transcribe Burchard's sermons for publication. Russell Streeter's *Mirror of Calvinistic, Fanatical Revivals* had cast Burchard in such a repulsive form while broadcasting Woodstock's (or at least the town fathers') low opinion of the revivalist, that Burchard and his supporters, suspecting Marsh and other university people of plotting another episode in the campaign to defame him, took countermeasures.

First Burchard tried to make a convert of B. J. Tenney in order to "extract the notes from him," and failing in that endeavor, then attempted to purchase his silence by "offering him a large sum" of money rumored to be "more than 150 dollars." Pretending to sell his notes, "Tenney pocketed the money," but did not surrender them. Burchard feared the publication of transcripts of the meetings and next suggested that

the deacons physically restrain Eastman from taking notes. He
also urged President Bates, who had travelled to Williston for
the occasion, to denounce the students from the pulpit. Totally
frustrated in his attempts to prevent the note taking, Burchard,
as a last recourse, tried "to foil them . . . by holding his tongue"
and refused to preach when the offensive students were present.
His silence provoked "the great vexation of his followers," who
became "mad because they came to see the elephant, and the
elephant won't play off for fear his tricks shall be noted down."

Burchard's enraged disciples pinned responsibility for the affair on Goodrich, James Marsh, and the faculty of the University
of Vermont who had openly expressed their disdain for the
measures, calling them "fanaticism" or a deplorable "infatua-
tion which has seized our churches." "What is in store for the
College," wrote professor Torrey's worried wife, "I do not know—
but fear a storm is pending—There is great bitterness of feelings
towards the faculty (particularly Mr. Marsh) for the part they
took in reference to Burchard." Leaders of the revivalist faction,
such as the merchant Samuel Hickok, who had sponsored the
resolution that invited Burchard to Burlington, claimed that
publication of the notes would be tantamount to proof of the
faculty's guilt in the affair; and in such circumstances it would
be "their duty to withdraw their patronage from an institution
one of the teachers of which was engaged in so base a transaction."
While the storm blew itself out shortly after Burchard moved on,
the revival movement had provoked a debate of great importance.[37]

The reason contemporaries often stated for their opposition
to Burchard's revivals was that the introduction of large numbers of new converts to the church by the New Measures threatened the structure and meaning of Congregationalism as a holy
community. While the anti-Burchardites believed that the Congregational Church was a truly democratic institution, they
generally felt that Burchard's converts paid too little of themselves as a price for participation in that democracy. The commitment to Christ made while gingerly perched on an "anxious
seat" in the heat of a revival, they charged, could hardly endure
the cooling aftermath of day-to-day Christian experience, especial-

ly if that experience ever called for any sacrifice of those emotions aroused by the revival. For instance, one critic reported
to James Marsh that the questions asked by Burchard of the
tenants of the "anxious seats" hardly tested the depth of the
conversion. "Do you prefer going to meetings to going to shows
and balls . . . ?" he asked one anxious sinner in Burlington. Hardly a searching question to put to an excited person being examined for church membership, Burchard's critics charged. Instead,
they claimed that the time for examination should be when one's
intellect and emotions are in harmony, a moment seldom observed
at a meeting led by Jedidiah Burchard.[38] The pastors of the Rutland Association found the revival contained "too little to en-
lighten the mind, awaken and invigorate the power & authority
of the conscience." Instead, they commented disparagingly, "the
system of measures [was] adopted, + a variety of motives urged
for the purpose of exciting the mind to immediate action" rather
than evoking "the sober reflection of men acquainted with the
truths of spiritual religion."[39]

Moreover, as one report claimed, Burchard's converts were so
young or so ignorant as not to understand the full implications
of questions the revivalist asked about their spiritual state at
the moment of conversion.[40] Cheap prices buy cheap goods,
the anti-Burchardites argued; and if church membership is cheap-
ly bought, its value is depreciated.

In response to his critics in Burlington, probably members
of the University of Vermont's faculty, Burchard retorted in a
sermon:

The Church has been deceived by the devil, and talks about
giving people time *to think*. That's all nonsense. Men won't
think. . . . Let any good minister, even Br. Smithgate of this
church [in Williston], preach the doctrines of the gospel ever
so plainly, from Sabbath to Sabbath, and then tell sinners to
think upon the subject of salvation, and make up their minds
cooly: and how many would be saved by their *thinking*? How
many? Why, common sense teaches that he wouldn't save one
in a month. I tell you, *people won't think. They are too dull*

and lazy to think! They want *excitement*. I have found by
several years experience that sinners are converted by being
excited. That's what we have the *anxious seats* and *general
prayers* for. It's to call down the Holy Ghost right into their
souls, and excite them to inquire,—Master, Jesus Christ—the
Almighty God, what shall I do to be saved from endless hell.[41]

Those Congregationalists who held the orthodox, though perhaps elitist, view of their churches as democratic communities in
which full participation was dearly bought, greatly feared that the
heated and acrimonious argument surrounding the revivals would
split their churches and in the guise of spiritual democracy weak-
en both their community and the "real" democracy along with it.
From Germany and France, with the breadth of the Atlantic
Ocean to promote objectivity, University of Vermont Professor
of Languages Joseph Torrey warned his wife to exercise a good
measure of forbearance to prevent a serious split in the church.
"When from this great distance I look back to Burlington . . . I
can easily overlook the misguided zeal of a few individuals, and
convince myself they mean right after all. I hope you all feel just
as I do," he continued. "If you do there will yet be no breach in
the church, and in a short time, all will look back upon the whole
matter with the same sentiments."[42]
   In 1831 when Asahel Nettleton had brought New Measures to
Hartford, Connecticut, similar criticisms, lodged against him and
those he converted, convinced them of the need to establish a
new, separate congregation, which they called the Free Church
of Hartford. The original congregation of the Free Church of
Hartford consisted of thirty-three members of Hartford's population. With pews and membership free, unlike other churches in
the city, its membership was open to all who sought it. Intensely
democratic, the Free Church grew in membership to two hundred
soon after its founding in 1832 and at the same time became the
focal point in Hartford for the discussion and support of the
major liberal causes of the mid-thirties. Eventually, however,
membership declined, curiously enough because of objections
to free pews. Apparently some church members there too came

to think that cheap prices bought cheap goods. In any event, the
Free Church dissolved as a free church in 1838, charged pew rent,
and reorganized as the Fourth Congregational Church of Hartford.[43]

In Vermont, despite serious threats, no successful counter-
congregations actually resulted from Burchard's New Measures.
The nearest thing in Vermont to Hartford's Free Church came
in an attempt by John Truair, the prophetically named Congregational minister in Fletcher, to found the Union Church of
Christians in 1833. Dismissed from the Northwest Association of
Congregational Ministers because of his Swedenborgian professions, Truair founded a congregation which tried, like Burchard,
to avoid the sectarian professions of Congregationalists, Methodists, Baptists, and Episcopalians, the major Protestant sects in
Vermont at the time. He achieved little success with the Union
Church of Christians, however, even in Fletcher, where, the
town's historian noted with superior sarcasm some thirty years
later, Truair's Union Church lived about as long as Jonah's
gourd.[44]

Unlike the early supporters of the Free Church in Hartford
or Truair's Union Church of Christians, members of the University of Vermont faculty, the Rutland Association, and other
detractors did not acknowledge Burchard's revivals as a democ-
ratizing force in Vermont life. Instead they saw the New Measures as a threat to what many believed was the oldest social
and religious institution in New England, the Congregational
Church. "It seems to me," James Marsh said in a lengthy letter
written to President Nathan Lord of Dartmouth College in late
1835, ". . . that [Burchard] tends, with direct and irresistible
force, to do that for the church, which sheer jacobinical radical-
ism will do for the State, . . . may God preserve his Church!"[45]
For many of those most staunchly against the revivals, their opposition not only comprehended theological matters, it also
rested on their concept of the proper organization of society.
The Rutland Association was convinced that "the system of
measures" could not help but diminish "the ordinary ministra-
tions of the Gospel, upon the sound sense and the enlightened
conscience of the community at large."[46]

The main points of James Marsh's criticism of Burchard's
measures were thus both social and theological. Burchardism,
Marsh first argued, strayed from the intellectual rigor and emotional purity of traditional evangelical religious revivalism as
expressed by such religious writers of the seventeenth and eighteenth centuries as John Bunyan or David Brainerd, whose
spiritual journal Jonathan Edwards had published. In both Bunyan's *Pilgrim's Progress* and Brainerd's *Journal,* just as in the
religious discourses of such seventeenth-century English divines
as Henry More, Isaac Barrow, and John Bates, Marsh pointed out,
there could be found clear expressions of profound spiritual
humility and emotional emptiness as conditions of conversion,
conditions hardly possible in the face of Burchard's vigorous
and vulgar self-assertiveness. Moreover, Marsh found Burchard's
Biblical knowledge and critical intellect inadequate to the task
he set out to perform, a conclusion firmly proven, Marsh said,
when the spirited evangelist answered a question about how
Peter reckoned a figure of three thousand converts on a single
occasion by saying that the Apostle counted his converts in the
same way as Burchard did himself, by dividing them into sheep
and goats.

The most damaging criticism against Burchard in the eyes of
Professor Marsh, who was recognized at the time as the leading
American spokesman for Samuel Taylor Coleridge's spiritual
philosophy, was that Burchard's measures for conversion lacked
any truly spiritual dimension. Instead Burchard's revival meetings played on the mass emotions of congregations and brought
attendants at "protracted meetings" to a sense of conversion
largely through the compulsion of mass emotional outpourings.
Such measures, Marsh charged, relied on materialistic mass
psychology and certainly not the workings of the Holy Spirit.
Because of what he considered the transitory nature of mani-
pulated emotions, Marsh saw the New Measure revivals as a
threat to the very basis of the established church, for they
brought to the church new members who lacked the deep, uni-
fied emotional and intellectual commitment which the church
community needed to sustain itself and even survive.

Marsh thought his anxiety over the future of Congregational-

ism in Vermont after Burchard's converts had been admitted to
church membership was warranted in light of the experience
in Rochester, New York, a few years earlier during a revival
there. Marsh's fears were well based, for the meaning of Congregationalism and the role it would play in Vermont society
underwent a serious test in 1835-36, just as Presbyterian churches
in Rochester had been tested earlier in the decade. The Great
Revival led by Charles Grandison Finney at Rochester, a city of
ten thousand in the late 1820s, produced, according to reports,
converts in the range of two to three thousand souls, thus en-
larging the rolls of the city's Presbyterian churches threefold.
But within five years, the enthusiasm of conversion had dissipated
and the holy communities had fallen into disarray. Marsh knew
of the experience of the church in Rochester from friends on the
faculty of Auburn Theological Seminary and from a colleague
on the faculty of the University of Vermont, Farrand Benedict,
whose father, Abner Benedict, had been pastor of a church in
Rochester. So he feared the same results in Vermont from
Burchard's revivals.

Another event closer to home a few years earlier in towns
north of Burlington could equally have frightened Marsh and
strengthened his opposition to Burchard. When a revival led
by the itinerant Reverend Davidson swung through Fairfield,
Bakersfield, Milton, Georgia, Fairfax, and parts of Grand Isle
County in the islands of Lake Champlain, many citizens of
that northwestern corner of the state thought they were hearing the voice of a true prophet among them. Especially after
one of Davidson's new converts, a Mrs. Thompson, leaped to
her feet during a sermon by Davidson and declared herself the
newly risen Christ, some, including Davidson himself, were
convinced that the Second Coming had brought the Savior to
Vermont.

Mrs. Thompson gathered her disciples and toured the region,
presenting herself as the Christ come to preach a message from
God the Father. A curious message, indeed, it led some of her
more zealous followers to murder their children and themselves
commit suicide. The enthusiasm of Mrs. Thompson's revival

eventually abated, however, after Davidson was tarred, feathered, and run out of town facing backward on a small French horse. Mr. Thompson soon succeeded in capturing his wife from her disciples and effecting her incarceration in Saint Albans.[47] Fresh memories of Davidson's revivals and Mrs. Thompson's activities north of Burlington in 1830, as well as reports of events in Rochester, then, could have caused Marsh to fear similar results from Burchard's activities in 1835.

Marsh's concerns were well-founded in some respects, for the social energies of Vermont were not ultimately dominated or organized and directed through the Congregational or any other church after the mid-1830s, but instead through other means, such as the growth of the antislavery movement, the development of an embryonic labor movement in the Connecticut River Valley, and migration to the West. The experiences of the Baptists in Vermont during the entire decade of the 1830s, for example, in some important ways mirror the experiences of the Congregational churches of 1835-36 and seem to further confirm James Marsh's fears for the church as a social institution.[48]

Before 1830 new members were not coming to Vermont's Baptist churches in numbers that indicated a prosperous future for the church. Indeed, some congregations, like the First Baptist Church of Shaftsbury, saw a gradual decline in numbers from one hundred sixty after the War of 1812 to sixty-five by 1824. Then, in the 1830s, new members began to come into the fold. At the Fourth Baptist Church of Shaftsbury, after revivals in 1828 and 1831, seventy-three new members came in. The First Baptist Church of that town brought in forty in 1831 and seventy-two in the period 1831-34. Again in 1839 the Fourth Baptist Church called for a series of meetings, with Joseph Sawyer, an itinerant revivalist, leading them; fifty new members came into the church (*BV*, pp. 61-63).

The feelings of helplessness that seemed to impel congregations to hold revivals are suggested in the account of a meeting at the Baptist Church of East Hubbardton in the grim, deep winter month of February 1830. Briefly before this date the

congregation "had given up their meetings in despondence."
A few remaining members gathered that February, "mourning
over the low estate of Zion," and decided to try "to stir each
other up" through a revival. On the appointed meeting day
only five members and two neighboring women, "one of them
an Irish woman," gathered at the church. "Gloom and sadness
brooded over the meeting though the time was spent in prayer
and a free exchange of feeling in view of the low state of Zion."
Just before breaking up in discouragement, the nonmember
women were given an opportunity to speak, and the Irish woman, to everyone's surprise, "related a Christian experience full
of thrilling interest" and expressed a wish to be baptized, as
did the woman with her. "The brethren were melted into tears
. . ." and a general revival followed soon thereafter in East Hubbardton, an event of such enthusiasm that the ice had to be cut
from a local pond to allow open water for baptisms (*BV*, pp.
92-93).

By 1835 the Baptist State Convention had developed a mis-
sionary movement in Vermont, and maintained until 1840 seven
missionaries each year throughout the state and the bordering
townships of Canada. In 1838 six missionaries from Vermont
were especially appointed to the Canadian border mission fields.
Led by Edward Mitchell and Jonathan Baldwin, with financing
provided by the State Convention, the itinerant Baptist revivalists commenced their mission after a protracted meeting at Saint
Albans in 1838. They were finally able to report the establishment in Canada of nine churches with four hundred members
(*BV*, pp. 455-57).

Throughout the decade revival enthusiasm burned in Baptists
across Vermont. Pownal in the midsummer of 1834 held a protracted meeting and revival that brought fifty-nine new members
to the church. In Manchester in 1838 a series of meetings in
July brought daily baptisms. Windsor from 1829 to 1833 held
"a continuous revival," with weekly baptisms resulting in one
hundred thirty new members. "Four successive revival years in
Addison" were initiated in 1831. The new Baptist Church of
Burlington doubled membership between June 1835 and July
1836. Concurrently the Baptists founded schools: Brandon

Academy (1831); Leland and Gray (1835) in Townshend;
Black River Academy (1834) in Ludlow; and, at a site selected
because of its proximity to Canadian mission fields, Derby
Academy in 1839 (*BV*, pp. 537-43).

But by 1841, both the spiritual and temporal fortunes of
Vermont's Baptist churches had begun to decline. At the
State Convention of 1841 the Committee on the State of
Religion reported: "There has been [a] general dearth of revival intelligence through the state. . . . This is one of the most
unfavorable indications in the history of the Baptist denomi-
nation in this state" (*BV*, p. 458). The convention found its
treasury so small in 1841 that it had to decline nearly all ap-
plications for aid to churches. By 1843 no missionaries were
employed. "Even the Canadian mission was cut off" and aid to
Canadian churches withdrawn (*BV*, p. 459). The 1840s were,
in the words of the church's historian, "that disastrous decade
when many of our churches were becoming extinct" (*BV*, p. 207).

What James Marsh and his fellow critics of the revivals could
not anticipate, however, was the way the reaction to the *patriote*
rebellions in Lower Canada would pick up the slack in Vermont
when the revivalist enthusiasm of 1835-36 began to wane in 1837
after Burchard led his revival troupe back to New York State
and up the southwestern shore of Lake Champlain. When he came
to recognize how the activities of the loud *patriote* supporters
in Vermont paralleled the behavior of Burchard's disciples and
converts, Marsh, as well as other prominent figures in Burlington,
quickly mounted a campaign against American support of the
patriotes and entered into a vigorous debate with their Vermont
supporters during the winter of 1837-38.

Implicit in their antagonism to eager adoption of the *patriote*
cause by many Vermonters was a continued fear of what Marsh
described to Nathan Lord as the Jacobinical message of Burchard's
revival. For Marsh and other like-minded Vermonters, both the
revivals and the philo*patriote* movement would lead to a radical
destruction of the state's and the nation's social fabric. Bishop
John Henry Hopkins, a High Churchman with well-developed
elitist principles and affinities for John Henry Newman and the
Oxford Tractarians, had been a harsh critic of revivals for reasons

similar to Marsh's. In late 1837 he left Vermont for London on a
campaign to raise money for his Vermont Episcopal Seminary.
Soon after his arrival in England, however, Hopkins encountered
the radical reformer Robert Owens, whose socialistic principles
Hopkins found just as irreligious and "destructive of the existing
order of society" as Burchard's revivals had been a few years
earlier in Vermont. Having been first appalled by the "leveling"
tendencies of Owens's plans for redistributing power and wealth,
Hopkins was then equally embarrassed by reports of Vermont's
enthusiasm for the *patriotes* during a debate in Parliament on the
recent uprising in Canada. He noted in his diary that the philo-
patriotes were doubtless drawn from the lowest levels of society
(an erroneous assumption) and their behavior only a temporary
social aberration. He was far more comfortable later in May
1838, during a dinner at the Archbishop of Canterbury's residence, when Lord Gosford, recently returned from his troubled
governorship in Canada, greeted him warmly, praised him for
the sermon delivered at Quebec a few years earlier, and "was
exceedingly kind and sociable."[49]

But for those Americans drawn to Burchard's and other revivals throughout the country, the message delivered from the
pulpit during "protracted meetings" promised salvation from
the social and personal dilemmas intensely felt during the 1830s.
The Great Revival, including Burchard's New Measures version,
swept through the country offering a cohesive focus in an apparently diffusive moment in time. Men and women were drawn
to the "anxious seats," and the union with other new converts
that followed, in pursuit of a purpose they equated with their
own national and communal ideal of liberty and improvement.
The Burchard revival was symptomatic of the unrest of the 1830s
and of a people eagerly seeking answers and new solutions to the
problems that vexed them.

NOTES

1. Captain Frederick Marryat, *Diary in America*, ed. by Jules Zanger,
(Bloomington, Ind., 1960), 166-170.

2. Along with Mrs. Trollope and Captain Marryat, most English travellers
of the period rushed "to the defense of old English institutions by an attack

on American democracy" (Allan Nevins, ed., *American Social History As Recorded by British Travellers* [New York, 1923], 122, and their observations, while biased, recorded the turmoil in the bumptious American 1830s. See, for example, Charles Dickens, *American Notes for General Circulation* (Boston, 1867); J. S. Buckingham, esq., *America, Historical, Statistic, and Descriptive,* 3 vols. (London and Paris, 1841); or Thomas Hamilton, *Men and Manners in America,* 2 vols. (London, 1833).

3. Francis Trollope, *Domestic Manners of the Americans* (London, 1832), quoted in Allen Nevins, ed., *America Through British Eyes* (New York, 1948), 83. Hereafter cited parenthetically. "Fanny Trollope did several things worth remembering. She wrote a rude book about America (*Domestic Manners of the Americans*) and a poor novel about English industrial life (*Michael Armstrong*), both of which were popular successes, and she had a son who very nearly became one of the great novelists of his age." (Peter Keating, "Victorian Lives," *Times Literary Supplement,* December 7, 1979, p. 90.)

4. H. L. Mencken's *The American Language* (New York, 1937), 300-303, also recounts the experiences of Captain Marryat and Mrs. Trollope in the 1830s when they encountered the, by then, fully blossomed American prudery in language usage. When Captain Marryat in 1837 asked a young lady at Niagara Falls if her leg were hurt after slipping, she told him that a leg was never mentioned before ladies; the proper word was limb. Even chickens ceased to have legs.

5. Hamilton, *Men and Manners,* II, 394.

6. *See,* for example, John R. Bodo, *The Protestant Clergy and Public Issues, 1812-1848* (Princeton, N.J., 1954); Charles Foster, *An Errand of Mercy: The Evangelical United Front, 1790-1837* (Chapel Hill, 1960); Charles G. Cole, Jr., *The Social Ideas of the Northern Evangelists, 1820-1860* (New York, 1954); Gregory H. Singleton, "Protestant Voluntary Organizations and the Shaping of Victorian America," in Daniel W. Howe, ed., *Victorian America* (Philadelphia, 1976); and Donald G. Mathews, "The Second Great Awakening as an Organizing Process, 1780-1830, *American Quarterly,* 21 (1969), 22-43.

7. Mathews, "Second Great Awakening," 26-31.

8. Ibid., 27.

9. Zadock Thompson, *History of Vermont, Natural, Civil, and Statistical* (Burlington, Vt., 1842), Pt. II, 93.

10. Nathan Haskins, *A History of the State of Vermont* (Vergennes, Vt., 1831), 18-19.

11. *See* T. D. S. Bassett, "Irish Immigration to Vermont Before the Famine," *Chittenden County Historical Society Bulletin,* No. 4, (March 1966). Travelling through Burlington in 1835, Nathaniel Hawthorne spoke for many nativists when he observed at Burlington's harbor a "swarm" of Irish, a third part of whom could not earn "a daily glass of whiskey . . . doubtless their first necessity of life."

12. Samuel Swift, *History of the Town of Middlebury* (Middlebury, Vt., 1859), 98.

13. Jedidiah Burchard remains an elusive figure in the history of the Great Revival of the 1830s in northern New York and western New England. The little published information about him that survives can be found in Whitney R. Cross, *The Burnt-Over District: The Social and Intellectual History of Enthusiastic Religion in Western New York 1825-50* (Ithaca, 1950), 188-89; Frank G. Beardsley, *A History of American Revivals* (New York 1904), 161-62; William F. Noble, *God's Doings in Our Vineyard* (Philadelphia, 1882), 401-6; H. Pomeroy Brewster, "The Magic of a Voice," Rochester Historical Society Publications Fund Series, 4 (1925), 273-90; David Ludlum, *Social Ferment in Vermont, 1791-1850* (Montpelier, Vt., 1937), 56-57; and Nell Jane Barnett Sullivan and David Kendall Martin, *A History of The Town of Chazy, Clinton County, New York* (Burlington, Vt., 1970), 226.

14. Comings MSS, UVM Archives, Burlington, Vt., Elam J. Comings to [Fanny?], April 25, 1835; and Torrey MSS, UVM, Mrs. Torrey to the Reverend Joseph Torrey, Burlington, January 19 and 20, 1836.

15. *Records of the First Congregational Church in Burlington* (Burlington, Vt.), II, 71.

16. Ibid., 70. The church called the protracted meeting and invited Burchard to conduct it on August 22, 1835. The meeting actually commenced on December 8.

17. Sullivan and Martin, *History of Chazy*, 226.

18. *Records of the First Congregational Church in Burlington*, II, 71.

19. Comings MSS, UVM, Elam J. Comings to Capt. A. Comings, Burlington, December 23, 1835.

20. *Records of the First Congregational Church in Burlington*, II, 71.

21. Torrey MSS, Mrs. Torrey to Rev. Joseph Torrey, Burlington, January 19 and 20, 1836.

22. Comings MSS, UVM, Elam J. Comings to Capt. A. Comings, Burlington, December 23, 1835.

23. Russell Streeter, *Mirror of Calvinistic, Fanatical Revivals, or Jedidiah Burchard & Co. During a Protracted Meeting of Twenty-Six Days, in Woodstock, Vt. to which is added the "Preamble and Resolution" of the Town Declaring Said Burchard a Nuisance to Society* (Woodstock, 1835).

24. George Perkins Marsh MSS, Dartmouth College Library, Hanover, N.H., Marsh to father (Charles Marsh), Burlington, December 29, 1835.

25. Minutes of the Rutland County Association of Congregational Ministers, February 2, 1836, VHS Collections, Montpelier, Vt.

26. Ibid.

27. For Charles G. Eastman's report of how the minister and the congregation in Williston sympathetically received Burchard *see* Charles G. Eastman, ed., *Sermons, Addresses and Exhortations of Jedidiah Burchard* (Burlington, Vt., 1836), App., 108-10.

28. George Perkins Marsh MSS, Marsh to father, Burlington, December 29, 1835. Marsh noted that "Professors Hough, Turner of Middlebury, agree in opinion with Mr. [James] Marsh and Mr. Wheeler." He also suggested sarcastically that Burchard's support from "the friends of Middlebury College" came "for the laudable purpose, no doubt, of building up the one institution at the cost of the other."

29. Comings MSS, UVM, Elam J. Comings to Capt. A. Comings, Burlington, December 23, 1835.

30. George Perkins Marsh MSS, George Perkins Marsh to father, Burlington, December 29, 1835.

31. Ibid.; Marryat, *Diary in America*, 140.

32. Minutes of the Rutland County Association of Congregational Ministers, Brainerd [?] Kent, Joseph Hurlburt, and Henry P. Hickok to Chittenden County Association, March, 1836, VHS Collections, Montpelier, Vt.

33. Torrey MSS, Mrs. Torrey to Rev. Joseph Torrey, Burlington, January 19 and 20, 1836.

34. Benedict MSS, UVM, G. W. Benedict to E. C. Benedict, Burlington, January 23, 1836.

35. Comings MSS, UVM, Elam J. Comings to Capt. A. Comings, Burlington, December 23, 1835.

36. Streeter, *Mirror of Calvinistic, Fanatical Revivals*.

37. The episode of trying to thwart Burchard by publishing accounts of his sermons and the meetings has been derived from Eastman, *Sermons, Addresses and Exhortations of Jedidiah Burchard*, App.; Benedict MSS, G. W. Benedict to E. C. Benedict, Burlington, January 23, 1836; and Torrey MSS, Mrs. Torrey to Rev. Joseph Torrey, Burlington, January 19 and 20, 1836, and Rev. Joseph Torrey to Mrs. M. N. Torrey (wife), Bonn, Germany, January 6, 1836, and Paris, France, March 1, 1836.

38. *CAD*, 177, 189, James Marsh to Nathan Lord, December 1835.

39. Minutes of the Rutland County Association of Congregational Ministers, VHS Collections, Montpelier, Vt.

40. The wife of John Wheeler, president of UVM, reported to Marsh that Mrs. Burchard led a revival of Burlington children in the same manner as Burchard did with the adults. Marsh told Nathan Lord that she "induced a collection of nearly a hundred to say . . . that they had given their hearts to God . . . there was but one face among them that showed any peculiar solemnity." *CAD*, 189, James Marsh to Nathan Lord, December, 1835.

41. Eastman, *Sermons, Addresses and Exhortations of Jedidiah Burchard*, 33.

42. Torrey MSS, Rev. Joseph Torrey to Mrs. M. N. Torrey, Bonn, Germany, January 6, 1836, and Paris, France, March 1, 1836.

43. *Memorial Manual of the Fourth Congregational Church, Hartford, Connecticut* (Hartford, 1882), 1-21. The Free Church Movement grew out of Charles Grandison Finney's revival activities and resulted in Free Churches being established in many of the major eastern cities such as Boston, New

Haven, and New York. They were formed, as members of the Free Church
of Hartford professed, "with the view of providing the means of grace
for the neglected and the increasing population of the city" (p. 8).
Antinomian controversy and "many erratic and extreme characters"
were eventually seen as threats to the church which could only be
averted by charging pew rent (p. 14).

44. Abby Hemenway, ed., *Vermont Historical Gazetteer* (Burlington, 1871), II, 210. *See also* Ludlum, *Social Ferment*, 249.

45. *CAD*, 183.

46. Minutes of the Rutland County Association of Congregational
Ministers, VHS Collections, Montpelier, Vt.

47. The story of Davidsonism and the following account of the Baptist
experience in Vermont during the 1830s is taken from Henry Crocker,
History of the Baptists in Vermont (Bellows Falls, Vt., 1913), cited parenthetically hereafter as *BV*.

48. Ludlum, *Social Ferment*, 155-66, points out that after 1837
the abolition question severely distressed Congregational, Methodist, and
Episcopal churches in Vermont. Not until the late 1840s would the General
Convention of Congregational Ministers in Vermont declare mildly that
slavery was "utterly sinful before God" (*Extracts from the Minutes of the
General Convention . . .* [1846]). E. C. and Joseph Tracy, editors of the
Vermont Chronicle, which William Lloyd Garrison called "the most ego-
tistical, the most querulous, and the most dangerous publication in New
England" (*Liberator*, January 4, 1831), led with James Marsh, until his
death in 1842, the opposition to the convention's formal denouncement
of slavery. Methodist and Baptist churches in Vermont experienced similar
internal controversies and during the mid-1840s underwent basic organiza-
tional ruptures over the question of abolition.

An early, but still important, study of population trends in northern
New England is Harold F. Wilson, "Population Trends in North-Western
New England, 1790-1930," *New England Quarterly*, 7 (1934), 276-77.

Ludlum also has a brief discussion of the social reform movements
of the 1840s (pp. 205-37) and their relations to the forces that compelled
migration after the Panic of 1837 (pp. 260-73). *See also* Louis D. Stilwell, *Migration from Vermont* (Montpelier, Vt., 1948). Stewart Holbrook's *The Yankee Exodus* (Seattle, 1950) still provides the best over-
view of New England migration.

49. Bishop Hopkins's record of his journey to England in 1837-38
is contained in a diary deposited in the library of VHS, Montpelier.

CHAPTER THREE

LES FRERES CHASSEURS:
A VERMONT TALE

Through one bitterly cold night in mid-December 1837, a group
of men stood watch at each of two bridges spanning the Winooski
River on the northbound roads out of Burlington, Vermont. Although some of the men, among them a son of the mill-owning
Catlin family, were important figures in the commercial life of the
busy, northern New England village, all of them were closely muf-
fled as much against the curious eyes of any passersby as against
the cold. Alec Catlin and his companions wanted to draw as little
attention as possible to their frigid evening's adventure on the road
to Montreal.

Meanwhile, in town keeping a similar watch for the same quarry,
Burlington's Constable Heyman Lane and Alec's father Guy Catlin stood across the street from the house of a French-Canadian
resident of Burlington, a blacksmith named Omer. They were
waiting for the smith to leave on what the watchmen thought a
suspicious and probably mischievous mission north into Canada.

Earlier in the week, Omer had made the rounds of Burlington's
livery stables trying to hire, according to a rumor following him,
a sleigh to drive him north to Montreal. The rumor moved swiftly
through Burlington, its transmission punctuated with a question:
why would a blacksmith, known to be in debt, want to take an

expensive and uncomfortable overland journey to Montreal—
unless someone else would pay handsomely for it? The suspicion
implicated Lord Gosford, Governor General of Canada, and held
that Omer had valuable information to sell Gosford about the
activities of the *patriotes* and their American sympathizers. In
November 1837, urged on by Louis-Joseph Papineau in the name
of liberty for French Canada, the self-styled *patriotes* launched an
armed insurrection in the British Province of Lower Canada. South
of the Canadian-United States border in Vermont, eager citizens,
fired by their memories of the American Revolution, adopted the
patriote cause. Their fervor led the Catlins and other supporters of
Papineau and defenders of liberty to stand watch three nights running in the middle of December in the hope of catching "Gosford's agent" in his flight northward.[1]

Close to one o'clock in the morning, suspicions and rumor
seemed about to come true. A sleigh drew up to Omer's house.
The blacksmith ran out, clambered into the sleigh, and drove off
across the snow packed streets of Burlington. He went south to
Middlebury, however, not north across the river toward Montreal.

Constable Lane and Guy Catlin, neglecting the men huddled on
the northern roads, then went home to their warm beds, while
their compatriots watched the bridges through the night. Having
invited frostbite and pneumonia as the thermometer registered
zero and the mists of the Falls of the Winooski swirled about
them, Alec Catlin and the other watchmen returned home to
breakfast in the first grey light that silhouetted the Green Mountains in the east.

That morning, recounting his part in the fruitless night watch
to his sons over the breakfast table, Guy Catlin told of watching
Omer ride off in the direction of Middlebury. As the full meaning
of his father's tale sank in, another son, Henry Catlin, who had
not been part of the night's adventure, leaped up from the table
crying, "What? Out of town to Middlebury? Why that man still
owes me five hundred dollars!"

In another time, when the political atmosphere would have
been less heated by agitation in support of the Lower Canadian
Rebellion of 1837, the Catlins might have appreciated Omer's

trick. *Les Frères Chasseurs*, a name soon to be adopted by American supporters of the Canadian rebels, or *patriotes* as they preferred, had failed to bag their game, losing five hundred dollars instead. In Montreal the night's escapade could have earned them the title *les chasseurs glacés*, just as in Vermont they became material for Yankee humor as the story of their night's exploits travelled through the town.

The story of the Catlins' night watch on the Winooski comes down to us in one version. Professor James Marsh, in a letter to his brother-in-law David Read, a Saint Albans attorney, recounted, with all the appropriate details, what he regarded as the foolish behavior of many of his fellow Vermonters.[2] Marsh had no sympathy for the *Patriote* War and thought that American support of it was a mistake. In a debate carried on through the mails between Read and himself during December and January, Marsh thoroughly discussed reasons for withholding support for the Canadian rebels and gleefully related the story of the Catlins' fruitless night watch to illustrate his position. Active support and sympathy on the one hand, and a fully articulated position of neutrality, though faintly suggesting hostility, on the other, were the dominant responses to the Canadian Rebellions. Marsh's account of the Catlins' exploits is thus doubly interesting; for it records not only one comic event in an epoch little understood and frequently ignored by American and even Vermont historians, but also, in its use in support of an earnest argument opposing such activities as the Catlins', clearly demonstrates the complexity of the American response to the *Patriote* War.

Indeed, in the series of events in Canadian-American relations clustered around the Rebellions of 1837-38, no episode comes more readily to hand than that of Alec Catlin's frozen watch by the Winooski. The attitudes and actions of many Vermonters ranging from the official to the completely unauthorized use of government property, are adumbrated in the Catlins' and Constable Lane's fruitless and frozen stakeout in "the cause of liberty." Tales of "Lord Gosford's agents in our midst"; rumored threats of war with England; plans to frustrate the Crown's reputed "despotism and bloody tyranny" over British subjects

who some Americans believed were following the glorious tra-
ditions and examples of the American Revolution; charges that
soldiers of the young Queen Victoria, British regulars and Canadian loyalists, posed a threat to the civil liberties and very lives
of Vermonters; noisy debates in town halls throughout Vermont
ending in public resolutions for sympathy with the *patriotes* and
vehement expressions of hatred for British "tyranny"; grand
plans to aid the *patriotes* with arms followed by the quick and
embarrassing loss of two cannon "liberated" from the Vermont
militia and used by the *patriotes* in a brief encounter with loyalist forces—all were common and sometimes comic elements in the
daily life of Vermont in late 1837 and on through 1838.

Yet Vermont was not the only place in the United States to
experience such events. Threatened violence, actual violence,
thwarted plots, financial loss, and comic confusion characterized
the roles of many American citizens during the time of the Canadian Rebellions. The actions of the Catlins, Constable Lane, and
their friends during that December night at first suggest a comic
tale out of Vermont folklore. But a larger view recognizes similar
patterns of behavior by many other Americans, indicating that
the story of American efforts to support the Canadian *patriotes*
reveals something significant not only about the Catlins and Vermonters, but also about the American people in general during
the 1830s. Moreover, the attitudes of those Americans opposed
to support for the *patriotes* are equally revealing. Given certain
facts of the time and of the place, an examination of the story of
American reactions to the *patriotes* casts light on how men like
the Catlins, James Marsh, David Read, and other Vermonters
perceived and understood themselves as part of a nation.

Though some students of Canadian history have attempted
to discount the Rebellions of 1837-38 as either comic interludes
or minor aberrations, most do not find them nearly so easily put
aside, seeing in them instead an important step in the path of
Canadian development and self-government.[3] Many French-
Canadian scholars have gone even further and viewed the rebellions in Lower Canada as part of the fight for national identity.
Moreover, important social, economic, and political reverbera-
tions in the United States and Canada have seldom paid heed

to the boundary that separates them. The Canadian-American relationship has been both intricate and close, with each people's or nation's role in that relationship defined in part by its own self-perceptions.

American responses to the small rebellion on the northern border in 1837-38 indicate a great deal about American self-perceptions in those years. With a small and relatively homogeneous population as yet untouched by much first generation foreign immigration in the first half of the nineteenth century, northern Vermont, as Alice Felt Tyler observed, was "entirely American."[4] Economic conditions in northern Vermont had never returned to the boom days of the turn of the nineteenth century and in comparison the commercial life of the 1830s had become stable and regularized. By 1830 the headlong rush of population that had made Vermont one of the fastest growing states had slowed down, and in the next decade the state's population grew barely 4 percent, compared to 32 percent across the nation. The fast-paced boom conditions and rough frontier atmosphere had gradually given way to the slower tempo of a more institutionalized, but not necessarily more stable, society. The dwindling forest could no longer support the risky native lumber and ash industries at the pace that had formerly made them the backbone of the Champlain Valley economy. Since these developments were coupled with evidence of exhausted soil, many in Vermont left their increasingly marginal farms for the West, or for small local industry. The Panic of 1837 and its aftermath harshly affected northern Vermont, though not with the devastating consequences found in other sections of the country.[5]

Publicly articulate and steeped in the tradition of New England's town meetings, its people spoke freely and often on internal, external, and, in a region where religious revivals dotted the landscape, eternal affairs. Among his many observations on America, de Tocqueville noted how the formation and influence of public opinion played an important role in the development of a democratic society. The traditional aristocratic network of controlling relations—an established church, social classes, a permanent community—tended to dissolve into ranks of free, but isolated, individuals. The American stood alone, responsive only to public opinion and the law as controls that replaced the networks of an aristocratic society. Newspapers, the common vehicle for spreading public opinion, were numerous and widely distributed within Vermont and, fortunately, have survived along with important public and private collections of documents from that period.[6]

The evidence contributes to a consistent view of one facet of a national identity in the early stages of its continuing process of development. In the disparate responses to the Canadian *Patriote* War, Americans carried on a dialogue or, perhaps more accurately, a debate with themselves. The debate was conducted both publicly in the newspapers, and privately in the correspondence of men like James Marsh and David Read, over such questions as the meaning and contemporary relevance of the American revolutionary experience of 1776, the nature of a neutral state and its responsibilities for the unofficial actions of its citizens, the meaning of liberty, the roles of individuals and the community in defining liberty in a democracy, and the implications of continental expansion.

Important questions concerning a nation's basic political philosophy and the individual's role and responsibilities within it tend to surface in times of social strain. Strained social conditions pertained nationally in 1837-38, as they had for much of the turbulent thirties. The relatively quiet interlude that followed the War of 1812, the Era of Good Feelings, allowed Americans to reflect on who they were and what they meant as a society. The repose gave way to the faster economic step of a dawning industrial age, massive social mobility, and the truculent rhetoric that characterized the Jacksonian era. The nation quickened its pace and entered the new era with the questions of identity, as yet unresolved, debated consciously by the new generation of American intellectuals and unwittingly in the popular outbursts and responses to the issues of the day.[7] It was a period of reform, of utopian ideas, of the Lowell girls in their idealized textile factory, of evangelical religion; and in Vermont, as David Ludlum's study of social ferment in the state amply and suggestively demonstrated, the existence of those same social conditions lends

weight to the view of Vermont as a paradigm of the national process of shaping a developing society.[8]

The actions of men like the Catlins, standing in the cold
through that December night in support of the cause of liberty,
represented both a participation in the process and a release
from its stresses. Uncertainties generated tensions and anxiety,
which in turn generated further uncertainties in a dismal cycle,
the resolution of which frequently came only through the as-
surance implicit in men uniting in action. That kind of action,
sought by the Catlins in mid-December 1837, reached fruition in
Vermont in 1838 with the formation of a secret society, *Les
Frères Chasseurs*, to bring the *patriotes'* supporters in the United
States and the Canadian exiles together for the purpose of planning the *patriotes'* and *liberty's* triumphant return to Canada.
Through 1838 they launched various unsuccessful military forays along the long Canadian-United States border in the passion-
ate hope of "liberating" Canada from British dominion.

All of the various Vermont responses to the *Patriote* War
reflect the larger national responses. *Les Frères Chasseurs*
or Hunters' Lodges organized all across the northern border
states and even into the South.[9] Buffalo and the Niagara
frontier witnessed the greatest *patriote* activities: large-scale
planning, recruiting, a camp on Navy Island, and several serious
raids. The American filibusterers at one point fell under the
questionable leadership of a "general" from one of New
York's oldest and most prominent families, Rensselaer Van
Rensselaer, son of a hero of the War of 1812, who joined the
Upper Canadian exile, William Lyon Mackenzie, at Buffalo
to organize American volunteers. Van Rensselaer helped to
lead at least one successful sortie against Canadian loyalist
forces in Upper Canada.[10] Governors William L. Marcy and
William H. Seward (elected in 1838) of New York and President Martin Van Buren recognized that the American volunteers on the Niagara frontier threatened to shatter already
fragile Anglo-American relations.[11] Though with great reluc-
tance to place their political ambitions athwart the popular

clamor for the liberation of Canada and retaliation for British
"outrages," Van Buren called for neutrality and dispatched troops
under General Winfield Scott to the Niagara frontier, while the
Canadian firebrand, Mackenzie, was jailed in Rochester.[12]

In Vermont *Les Frères Chasseurs* organized into lodges which
planned sorties into Canada and advertised in local newspapers
for recruits for a great "Wolf hunt." Prominent men like the
Catlins belonged to the lodges.[13] At the same time, however,
other leading citizens, though less often from the commercial
sector of the Vermont community and instead representing
the professions—lawyers, ministers, and faculty members of
the University of Vermont—stayed aloof from the *Patriote*
War and privately criticized American support for it. On one
notable occasion they took a public stand against American
supporters of the *patriotes* by publishing their petition to
Vermont's Governor Silas Jenison requesting that he declare
and enforce Vermont's neutrality, a declaration that Jenison,
like President Van Buren, cautiously promulgated.

Writing early in 1839 while Anglo-American relations were
still strained over the events of 1837-38, which included the
"Aroostook War" on the Maine-New Brunswick boundary, the
English poet William Wordsworth meditated in verse on the
reports of those riotous events. In a poem with a character-
istically long Wordsworthian title, "Composed on Reading an
Account of Misdoings in Parts of America," the poet wondered
where "in fate's dark book" lay the source of "this opprobrious
leaf of dire portent?" Did the original British colonists of North
America seek freedom only to pass on to later generations a
license "to passions turbulent" which gave "mutual tyranny a
deadlier look?" Recognizing those "Misdoings" as symptomatic
disturbances, however, Wordsworth then heard a softer voice
answering his question, instructing him to look below "the
stormy surface of the flood / To the great current flowing under-
neath. / . . . So shall the truth be known and understood."[14]
Attempts to explain the nature and origin of the strong, sometimes violent American responses to the *Patriote* War have tended
to examine only "the stormy surface of the flood" and thus

focussed on the argument that Americans flocked to the side of the *patriotes* because they had nothing better to do during the dreary depression-ridden winter of 1837-38. The usual reading of these events finds that the stagnating national economy in the wake of sudden deflation caused by the Panic of 1837 created large numbers of unemployed, particularly among the recently immigrated and reputedly rowdy Irish. Moreover, in and around Buffalo and Rochester an exceptionally large force of unemployed laborers, swelled by Erie Canal bargemen, stevedores, and Great Lakes sailors put out of work by the winter freeze-up, frequented the many taverns in search of work or to pass their idle days. Unemployed laborers, bargees, and sailors, including many Irishmen long infected with intense anglophobia, found an attractive prospect in the promise of a good fight against the hated British and maybe a little Canadian plunder.[15]

But such a reading hardly explains the leading presence of a Whig scion of the Rensselaer patroons at the head of a motley troop of bargees and stevedores, despite reports of certain disreputable aspects of the character of young "General" Rensselaer Van Rensselaer. Nor does it adequately answer the question of who in northern Vermont, where the effects of the Panic of 1837 were not as severe, supported the *patriotes*. With large-scale Irish immigration not yet begun, and with the hard times adding only a few to the seasonally unemployed sailors and freightmen along Lake Champlain, there was little basis for a social upheaval.[16] A second look at the principals in the comic plot to ambush one of "Lord Gosford's agents" suggests a different cast of characters.

First of all, Omer, the reputed spy, was a French Canadian who probably migrated from Lower Canada to Burlington. From the brief glimpse afforded by the story of his cunning escape from a debt, it seems that the liberation of Canada from British dominance held less import to Omer than the threat of a civil suit against him by Henry Catlin. Curiously, there is also little evidence that the one hundred or so other French Canadians who had migrated to Burlington before the great midcentury exodus from Lower Canada became involved in the activities south of the border in support of the *patriotes*.[17]

Instead, the evidence implicates the most substantial elements of society, prominent among them Henry Stacy, editor of the Burlington *Free Press*, and the Catlins, who owned a large mill on the falls of the Winooski River and provided employment for much of the French community of Burlington. In supporting the *patriotes* against the Crown and loyalist elements in Canada, the Catlins and their associates opposed their own economic self-interest. A significant portion of the Catlins' and other northern Vermont commerce involved trade with Canada, a trade that had flourished even during the turbulent days of the Embargo and the War of 1812.[18] But the major Canadian commercial firms and Canadian agents for the American merchants made up the vanguard of opposition to the *patriotes*. To support Louis-Joseph Papineau, Cyrile Coté, T. S. Brown, the Nelsons, and other *patriote* leaders was to oppose directly the Chateau Clique, the most powerful mercantile interests and the most rabidly anti-French group in Lower Canada. The motivation for the behavior of Vermonters like the Catlins transcends simply economic explanations.

When Wordsworth pointed in 1839 to a meaning in recent events in America lying somewhere below a turbulent surface, he demonstrated an understanding that psychologists have often acknowledged in poets, playwrights, and novelists. As Eric Erikson has observed, human behavior that "may appear to be the onset of neuroses, often is but an aggravated crisis which might prove to . . . contribute to the process of identity formation."[19] Particularly in relation to their responses to the *Patriote* War, citizens of Vermont both in withholding and offering aid to the Canadian rebels exhibit the characteristics of a people seeking an identity with the rest of their countrymen. It was a critical quest that America had been experiencing with varying intensity since the founding of the new nation.

NOTES

1. A standard synthesis of the events of the *patriote* uprising in Lower Canada is chapter four of Mason Wade's *The French Canadians, 1760-1945* (New York, 1955); for a brief review of the scholarship on the *patriotes*, see Chapter Four, "The Great Wolf Hunt," note 2.

2. MSS letter, James Marsh to David Read, December 21, 1837, photocopy in Wilbur Collection, UVM.

3. Three well-known Canadian historians, D. M. L. Farr, J. S. Moir, and S. R. Mealing, reflecting older historiography, wrote in their standard high school text, *Two Democracies* (Toronto, 1963), 144, that "the rebellions in the two Canadas did not really pose a serious threat to authority, and the events in Upper Canada especially had an almost comic opera appearance. Significantly, the population in both provinces did not support this resort to violence and the abortive rebellions were limited to the immediate vicinities of Montreal and Toronto." Many others regard the rebellions more seriously as an important nationalist movement and as events that helped usher in modern government and political life in Canada. Gerard Filteau in *Histoire des Patriotes*, (Montreal, 1938-42) I, 159, found the rebels neither democrats, reformers, nor liberals, but above all nationalists, who did not wish to overthrow institutions as much as they sought to employ them in the interests of the French-Canadian masses. A. R. M. Lower in *Canadians in the Making* (Toronto, 1958), 236, views the rebellions and subsequent disturbances as "parents of a new age" characterized by "the great historical swing" from the world of the eighteenth century to that of the nineteenth. See also below Chapter Four, note 2.

4. Alice Felt Tyler, *Freedom's Ferment: Phases of American Social History from the Colonial Period to the Outbreak of the Civil War* (New York, 1972), 68.

5. Reginald Charles McGrane wrote in *The Panic of 1837* (New York, 1965), 107, that Vermont "business and credit systems had received a serious shock," but "her citizens suffered less than those of other states." During the first months of 1837, the *Burlington Free Press* carried news of business failures in Vermont and New York, but on May 12, at the height of the Panic, the violently anti-Jackson newspaper assured its readers that Vermont was the state best prepared to meet the crisis caused by the financial "experiments of our tinkering tampering reckless rulers." Vermont banks also faired better than similar institutions in other states. With the notable exception of banks in Windsor and Essex, whose failures could be attributed more to mismanagement and illegal undercapitalization than to the Panic, Vermont banks had weathered the crisis by 1839. *See Vermont House Journal* (1838), App, XIX-XXX.

The data published by Thurston M. Adams, "Prices Paid by Vermont Farmers for Goods and Services and Received by Them for Farm Products, 1790-1940; Wages of Vermont Farm Labor, 1790-1940," *Vermont Agricultural Experiment Station Bulletin*, no. 507 (February 1944), demonstrate minor fluctuations in retail and wholesale prices.

6. By 1820 Vermont had twenty newspapers. Clarence S. Brigham, *History and Bibliography of American Newspapers, 1690-1820* (Worcester, 1947), II, 1070-1104.

7. The standard works on the United States and Vermont which discuss the causes and effects of various social factors in the development of

antebellum America are Alice Felt Tyler's *Freedom's Ferment* and David Ludlum's *Social Ferment in Vermont, 1791-1850* (Montpelier, Vt., 1948).

8. The War of 1812 marks an interesting and clear division in American intellectual life. From the end of the war to the mid-twenties are watershed years leading to a flowering of a new generation in letters, poetry, arts, education, and theology. The development lends substance to John Adams's famous comment that he would study the art of war so that his sons might study the art of politics, and their sons the arts.

Ludlum, *Social Ferment, passim.* Because of the scope of his study, Ludlum makes no specific examination of the years 1830-40; but the general picture of Vermont in that decade that emerges from his larger view of social conditions in the state supports our reading of Vermont in the 1830s.

9. The scholarship of *Les Frères Chasseurs* is very slim. Oscar A. Kinchen has written a monograph, *The Rise and Fall of the Patriot Hunters* (New York, 1956). See also the Abbé Ivanhoe Caron, "Une Société Secrète dans le Bas-Canada en 1838: L'Association des Frères Chasseurs," *Transactions of Royal Society of Canada*, 3rd Series, 20 (1926), 17-34; W. C. Overman, ed., "A Sidelight on the Hunter's Lodges of 1838," *Canadian Historical Review*, 19 (1938), 168-72; W. P. Shortridge, "The Canadian-American Frontier During the Rebellion of 1837," *Canadian Historical Review*, 7 (1926), 13-26; and Orris E. Tiffany, "The Relations of the United States to the Canadian Rebellion," *Publications of the Buffalo Historical Society*, 8 (1905), 1-147. Corey estimates that in 1838-39 Hunters' Lodges or *Les Frères Chasseurs* in the United States enrolled, as a conservative figure, forty to fifty thousand members. The *London Morning Chronicle* in 1841 reprinted a list of lodges from the *New York Journal of Commerce* which distributed lodges around the country as far from Canada as Louisiana (11 lodges), Virginia (21), Maryland (16), and Missouri (39). Vermont was said to have had 107 and New York 283. Albert B. Corey, *The Crisis of 1830-1842 in Canadian-American Relations* (New Haven, 1941), 75-76.

10. Rensselaer Van Rensselaer was a Whig political boss in his native Albany. While his father, General Solomon Van Rensselaer, had been a hero of the War of 1812, the son knew little military strategy or tactics and was described by an unfriendly contemporary as a "gin-sling, sottish-looking genius of twenty-seven." An account of Van Rensselaer's fruitless contributions to the *patriotes'* cause on the Niagara frontier, including his arrest and imprisonment by American authorities, is given in Corey, *Crisis,* 35-43.

11. On Van Buren's neutral position, cf. Corey, *Crisis,* 44-50 and 86. Corey also discusses Governors Marcy's and Seward's advocacy of reinforcing neutrality with military and naval forces, 154-55. One of the reasons Seward was able to defeat Marcy in 1838 related to the unpopularity of Marcy's neutrality stand. See Glyndon G. Van Deusen, *William Henry Seward* (New York, 1967), 52.

12. Corey, *Crisis*, 62-63 and 122; and William Kilbourne, *The Firebrand* (Toronto, 1956), 232.

13. The records of the Hunters' Lodges have not survived, but there is evidence of Alec Catlin contributing funds to the Canadian rebels and his membership in a lodge seems a safe surmise. *See* Catlin MSS, Wilbur Collection, UVM.

14. *The Political Works of William Wordsworth*, ed. by Ernest de Selincourt and Helen Darbishire (Oxford, 1947), IV, 137.

15. Corey, *Crisis*, 70 and 78; Kinchen, *Rise and Fall*, 63-64; Samuel Rezneck, "The Social History of the American Depression, 1837-1843," *American Historical Review*, 60 (1935), 662-87; and Blake McKelvey, "The Irish in Rochester: An Historical Retrospect," *Rochester History*, 19, no. 4 (October 1956), 4-5.

16. Significant Irish immigration came to Vermont and the Lake Champlain region after 1846. They generally arrived as construction hands when the railroad pushed north from Boston or on lake steamers from Lower Canadian ports. Bassett estimates a total Irish population in Vermont of about one thousand in 1830. See Harold F. Wilson, *The Hill Country of Northern New England* (New York, 1936), 40; Lewis D. Stilwell, *Migration from Vermont* (Montpelier, Vt., 1948), 196-197; and T. D. S. Bassett, "Irish Immigration to Vermont Before the Famine," *Chittenden County Historical Society Bulletin*, no. 4 (March 1966).

17. The French surnames scattered through the first volume of the Burlington Town Meeting Records and Bishop Plessis's visit to Burlington in 1815 (see Mason Wade, "The French Parish and *Survivance* in Nineteenth Century New·England," *Catholic Historical Review*, 36 [1950], 163-89) confirm the existence of a small French-Canadian community in Burlington. Yet there are very few local French names connected with the response to the *patriote* rebellion in either the newspapers or private correspondence.

18. H. N. Muller, III, "Smuggling into Canada: How the Champlain Valley Defied Jefferson's Embargo," *Vermont History*, 38 (Winter 1970), 5-21; and Catlin MSS, Wilbur Collection, UVM.

19. Erik Erikson, "The Problem of Identity," in *Identity and Anxiety*, ed. by M. P. Stern, A. J. Vidich, and D. M. White (Glencoe, Ill., 1960), 49.

CHAPTER FOUR
THE GREAT
WOLF HUNT

In the anxious atmosphere of the 1830s Vermonters watched
with great interest the events that unfolded to their north in
the troubled British colony of Lower Canada during the autumn
of 1837. The seeds of the troubles went back, perhaps, as far
as 1760, the time of the "conquest," when the British soundly
defeated the French and assumed control of the struggling colony
spread out along the banks of the Saint Lawrence River. At that
time French Canadians, suddenly leaderless and cast adrift in a
hostile English sea, found their traditional spiritual and commercial bonds with France abruptly severed. Devoted Catholics
became new subjects of a Protestant king and nation, but the
doughty *habitants* nevertheless persevered and multiplied. Stubbornly resisting repeated efforts at assimilation, they won recognition of their religion and quickly learned how to turn unfamiliar
English institutions into bastions to protect themselves.

By the early nineteenth century a French-Canadian majority
had firmly entrenched itself in the popularly elected assembly.
Representing a comparatively static, Catholic agrarian society

An earlier version of this chapter appeared as John J. Duffy and H. Nicholas
Muller, III, "The Great Wolf Hunt: The Popular Response in Vermont to
the *Patriotes* Uprising of 1837," *Journal of American Studies*, 8 (1974),
153-69. Reprinted by permission of Cambridge University Press.

cut off from most commercial outlets, they tried to resist the aggressive English-speaking society that gradually but inexorably encircled them. With equal determination, the British dominated the legislative council and the executive offices, while the Crown's omnipresent servant, the governor, occupied the Château Saint Louis, the traditional residence high on the rock at Quebec.

Soon fierce battles and a growing stalemate within the bosom of the colonial government reflected an increasing antagonism between the French and the English. The French saw the British not only as a serious threat to their traditional way of life, but also as an avaricious predator bent on exploiting resources properly belonging to future generations of French Canadians. The British, desperately wanting control of the lucrative promise of liberal capitalism and a transatlantic economy, steeped in a peculiarly Protestant ethic of progress, found French attitudes the antithesis of their ambitions. In sharp clashes over issues such as the tax structure, canal proposals, harbor improvements, or immigration policy, the arguments eventually focussed on the rights of the popularly elected assembly to govern as opposed to the Crown's prerogative.

This issue, exacerbated by devastating cholera epidemics, a series of agricultural disasters, chronic rural overpopulation, and the immediate economic distress and misery that followed the Panic of 1837, finally came to a head when Lord John Russell's infamous Ten Resolutions made it absolutely clear that the British had no intention of meeting any of the French majority's demands for reform. Under the uncertain but fiery leadership of Louis-Joseph Papineau, Drs. Robert and Wolfred Nelson, Dr. Cyrile Coté, Dr. E. B. O'Callaghan, Thomas Storrow Brown, and others, the *patriotes*, as the Canadian rebels called themselves, moved swiftly toward rebellion.[1]

On November 23, 1837, five companies of regular British infantry were routed by the ragtag *patriotes* in their stoutly defended village of Saint Denis on the east bank of the Richelieu River. The skirmish seemed to herald a bright future for the rebels, but their prospects dimmed considerably after crushing defeats at Saint Charles and Saint Eustache and the headlong

flight of the *patriote* leaders together with many of their followers south to the United States and safety.[2]

The fight at Saint Denis, the only *patriote* victory of the rebellion, marked the beginning of armed conflict that flared up
intermittently in Lower Canada until December 1838. The immediate and prevalent public response in Vermont, northern
New York, and all along the Canadian-United States frontier
was to acclaim the *patriotes* and to view the rebellion as a re-
enactment of the American Founding Fathers' own fight to
shake off British tyranny. In unabashedly adopting the rhetoric
of the American Revolution, the *patriotes* reinforced this view.
In the United States any fight involving the rights of a popular
assembly as opposed to the Crown, however superficial, evoked
a ready response. A public meeting in Barre typical of many convened in Vermont concluded "that the Patriots of Canada have
long been oppressed and deprived of their just rights, that like
our forefathers they have faithfully petitioned for a redress of
their wrongs, to the King and Parliament of Great Britain, and
having failed of redress, they are now justified in resistance to
the government which oppresses them."[3] Vermont still nurtured
a good deal of antipathy to the British. Memories of the Revolutionary War and British regulars billeted in the Hero Islands of
Lake Champlain, thirty miles south of the border, for nearly ten
years after the war, and the fresher memories of the battles of
the War of 1812 fought on the lake, could all stir up virulent
hatred toward "Tories" or whoever represented or wore the
British crown. The *Vermont Patriot*, in grossly erotic imagery,
wrote that the recently enthroned "Victoria is doubtless an
amiable and accomplished girl (Queen we should have said), and
as fit as almost any girl in Vermont of her age and capacity to
rule. But we do think it would be more modest (as well as convenient), in her royal majesty to keep her two pretty little feet
together somewhere on 'Britannia's Isle,' and not undertake to
place one on the Eastern and the other on the Western Conti-
nent. We don't fancy the idea of a female Colossus."[4] Speaking
more bluntly, the *Vermont Mercury* of Woodstock found the
Canadian Tories and their governor "rabid and unscrupulous

instruments" of British tyranny. "They are perfect bloodhounds," it continued, "growling and fretting for a year past . . . now unleashed [against the *patriotes*] and have a prospect of bathing their fangs in blood, they are wild and beside themselves with savage joy."[5]

Canadian affairs rapidly dominated the Vermont press, which appeared "unanimously favourable to the Patriot cause."[6] While skeptics properly questioned the unanimity of public opinion, and echoed Captain Marryat's remark about the Vermont editor who, "like most other editors in the United States . . . dared not put in anything which would displease his subscribers," the newspapers did reflect the general public support.[7] Their effusive pro-republican, anti-British rationale, which contained all of the mindless cant ritual required, masked more complex motives. Condemning at once Vermont newspapers and their leaders, Andrew Bell, another British observer, found support for the rebels in "the disrespectable sort of American papers." The support came from "vagabonds," he claimed, citizens "of a kind that the cities can well spare." The *patriote* cause attracted "fellows ripe for anything—the black sheep of different flocks— the refuse of respectable families. Any *row*, within a reasonable distance . . . will serve as a kind of seton to draw off much peccant humor from the body politic. It is all for liberty and glory— also," he added sardonically, "a little for pay and plunder— with these patriotic gentry."[8] The American response, however motivated, might have been purely academic had not the rebellion in Canada suddenly collapsed and turned to the American border towns for succor and financing, manpower, and military paraphernalia to renew the fight.

After their initial success in defending the village of Saint Denis, the rebels were badly defeated by the forces of the Crown at the Richelieu village of Saint Charles and the town of Saint Eustache in the Two Mountains district north of Montreal. As in most civil strife, conduct had gone far beyond the bounds of established rules of warfare, and no small amount of fear, hatred, and passion played upon the two groups now openly at

war within the bosom of Lower Canada.[9] The *patriote* rebellion collapsed for the time and most of the leaders and many
of the rank and file hastily fled southward to safety in New York
and Vermont. The excited and frightened postmaster of Henryville, just north of the Vermont border, with obvious relief reported that many of the *patriotes* had passed through his town
"without molesting us and are gone on to the South to procure
arms and to join the faction in Vermont."[10] After the severe
military reverses the rebellion ceased in its conventional military
form. Several ill-conceived filibustering expeditions issued from
Vermont and New York in the winter of 1837-38 and a general
uprising in November 1838, quickly crushed by the alerted
Canadian authorities employing British troops and loyal volunteers, as United States federal troops stood watch south of the
border, were the best the rebels could muster.[11]

In Vermont the rebels in exile found ready sympathy and
hardy approval for their cause. As had two previous generations
of Americans during the Revolution and the War of 1812, many
Vermonters boldly if naively talked of Canada as theirs only for
the marching. Willy-nilly they embarked on a disorganized attempt
to raise funds, arms, and supplies for the liberation of Canada.
Papineau, preceding his disciples to the United States, had already
been to Albany, where he conferred with Governor Marcy and
New York's Chancellor Dobsworth. He left there with the assumption "that he could borrow two hundred thousand dollars at New
York, Albany, Baltimore, Philadelphia and other places."[12] While
at Albany, according to one source, Papineau received offers from
both General Scott and General Wool not only "to command the
Canadians," but also "to bring with them a great number of sub-
altern officers, volunteers and soldiers" for the invasion of Canada.[13] The *patriotes* apparently neglected to act on this extraordinary offer and the generals soon received official orders to
go to the northern border in command of United States troops
sent to enforce American neutrality.

The military disasters and the flight from lower Canada ended
the notion of quick success and forced the *patriote* leadership
to reassess their situation and attempt to reorganize their follow-

ers. The Canadian fugitives held one of their most important con-
claves in January 1838 at Middlebury, Vermont, where Papineau,
who unsuccessfully tried to keep his presence a secret from the
public, and other leaders, including Dr. Robert Nelson, Dr. E. B.
O'Callaghan, and Thomas Storrow Brown, debated policy. Because of their disagreements on strategy, Papineau ceased to conduct further preparations against Canada, and the leadership
passed to Robert Nelson, "who till that time, had remained
quiet at Champlain [New York], but now felt compelled to
come forward and take command of the expedition which was
then organizing."[14]

Despite councils of the leadership, "organizing" for an expedition, and an elaborate secret association, *Les Frères Chasseurs*,
with its strict military structure, signs and passwords, and harsh
penalties for revealing secrets or disobeying orders, the *patriote*
exiles in northern Vermont and New York never marshalled their
resources efficiently nor kept their plans secret. Carrying two
standards made by the good ladies of Swanton and dragging their
borrowed cannon, a party of forty adventurers led by Dr. Coté
attempted to reenter Canada along Missiquoi Bay on December 6, 1837. News of their sortie preceded them, and they were
"ambushed by several hundred loyalists at St. Armands . . . with
the loss of one man killed, three wounded, one prisoner and their
two pieces of ordinance" before retreating to the safety of Swanton.[15] Even while Nelson planned the "major" assault from
Champlain, a mob of "50 or 60 desperados and pirates" went
off half-cocked (and probably half-drunk) at Troy, Vermont, and
at the cost of one of their number killed and three taken prisoner,
tried to help themselves to the Queen's arms.[16] While perhaps
providing an immediate release from tensions, these and other
ill-planned and ineffective excursions only dissipated the *patriote*
strength, demonstrated their hopeless lack of organization and
discipline, and cost them some support in both the United States
and Canada.

With the enthusiastic support of American sympathizers and
a highly successful raid on the United States arsenal at Elizabeth-
town, New York, the expatriates had less trouble assembling

arms. In Plattsburgh, at "the house of a man named Heath, a
marble cutter," the rebels made nearly eighty thousand car-
tridges.[17] In the meantime, contributions of small arms and
field pieces donated by individuals and town militias supple-
mented those stolen from the arsenal. McKeerman, a Canadian
tavernkeeper turned soldier, alone collected "more than fifty
stand" of rifles from Vermonters. "In St. Albans, Swanton,
Cambridge, and Johnstown [sic], there were gatherings of
arms, and . . . a single merchant in Johnstown [sic] contribute[d]
. . . five rifles at three pounds each to arm the Canadians." These
towns along with Montpelier and Middlebury also furnished cannon so that the rebels had at their "disposal nine or ten pieces."
Judge Gates of Cambridge personally gave arms to the *patriotes*
while Alec Catlin in Burlington lent his "generous assistance" in
money and storage facilities as well as arms.[18] After Nelson's
expedition had misfired and turned into the ignominious retreat
that characterized most rebel actions, General Wool carted off
fifteen hundred to two thousand captured rifles to the United
States arsenal at Vergennes, and the *patriotes* obligingly returned their cannon to the towns "under the promise," according to one rebel, "of allowing us to take them again; in case of
our resolving to re-attack Canada."[19]

The activities of the *patriotes* and their American supporters
had not been greeted with universal approbation in the United
States. In Washington President Van Buren, fearing the effect
of the events on the fragile state of Anglo-American relations,
dispatched General Wool to the tumultuous border and instructed United States district attorneys to "commence legal
proceedings against all such persons as appear to have been concerned in violating the law for preservation of the neutral relations." In addition the district attorneys were "to exercise constant vigilance during the pending contest, and to take all proper
steps to prevent the recurrence" of further violations of the
neutrality.[20] No evidence suggests any legal action was initiated
against Americans who supported the rebels, but in January and
February 1838, Daniel Kellogg, the district attorney from Rock-
ingham, Vermont, joined General Wool and scurried from town

to town along the border collecting information about rebel movements. Governor Jenison also joined Wool for one tour of the border on which Wool was disabused of his hope to use local militia to enforce neutrality. A group of volunteers from Sheldon, Vermont, presented themselves and awaited the general's orders. Testing their reliability, Wool enquired if they sympathized with the federal government or the radical *patriotes*. Their sergeant "unhesitatingly and with enthusiasm replied they were radical to a man. This was sufficient! The General ordered them to right about face and march home."[21]

Wool's and Kellogg's vigilance bore fruit on the nights of February 28, and on March 1, 1838, when they supplied intelligence that helped frustrate Nelson's abortive attack at Lacolle, six miles into Lower Canada, and captured many of the arms from the ragtag rebel army as it recrossed the border. Rushing back and forth between Burlington, Saint Albans, Plattsburgh, and Montpelier in February 1838, Kellogg wrote to his wife of the "sleepless vigilance" exercised "to preserve the neutrality upon this frontier." Kellogg hoped to preserve peace by "moral force" without "resort to the military" by giving "a proper tone to public sentiment and inculcating a due regard for the laws of the country." While in Plattsburgh he talked with Dr. Robert Nelson and found him "finely educated, highly intelligent and one of the most interesting men" he had ever met. Moral suasion failed to deter the rebel leader, however; and three days later Kellogg excitedly informed his wife that General Wool had sent to Vergennes for arms and was dispatching troops for the border.[22]

For the defeated *patriotes* the cause had been in deadly earnest, and many of them had unhappily committed their futures to it. One of their failures lay in their overestimation of the actual strength of American support. While the Americans raised a great ruckus and some arms and money, on the whole few made serious material sacrifices and fewer still were actually willing to march with the *patriotes*. Though they exhibited more vocal exuberance than is usually ascribed to normally taciturn Vermonters, few were so imprudent as actually to risk their lives. As one

boisterous Yankee in Saint Albans said, "I've a great mind to go
[and join the *patriotes*], but what I want is a good general to
take command; I want a Julius Caesar, or a Bonaparte, or a
Washington,—then I'll go!"[23] Clearly he would not march under
Dr. Robert Nelson, however much he might claim to support the
rebel leader.

But neither the *patriotes'* ultimate failure nor the measures
the United States government reluctantly adopted to preserve
neutrality were apparent in the excitement that attended the
enthusiastic welcome extended to the fleeing Canadian rebels.
In December 1837 and January 1838 the uproar created by the
patriotes' cause brought many Vermonters, in an archetypal
Yankee reflex, to a series of special public meetings held in towns
as widespread as Westford, Barre, Swanton, Burlington, Ludlow,
Northfield, Royalton, Danville, Middlebury, and Saint Albans.
Meetinghouses and churches were well packed with sympathizers
convened to express their opinions and to pass resolutions most
frequently drawn up by—as James Marsh, who offered no sympathy, lamented—"men in whom the great body of the community
place confidence."[24] The tenor and proceedings of the various
meetings were quite similar and wholeheartedly in favour of the
patriotes. In many cases the wording of the resolutions substantial-
ly reflected that from earlier meetings held in other towns. On
December 19, over two thousand freemen, according to an enthusiastic newspaper account, met in Saint Albans and adopted a
typical set of resolutions. They affirmed the inalienable rights
as set forth by Thomas Jefferson in the Declaration of Independence: "it ill becomes us to witness, with indifference, the conditions of such of the human family, as are struggling with patriotic zeal and in inequal circumstances to cast off the yoke of op-
pression . . . and that we ought . . . to countenance and encourage
that spirit, which will not obsequiously cower under, or crouch
to usurped power or tamely submit to violation of rights."[25]

The Saint Albans resolutions declared the intention to protect
the *patriotes* from the Tories' "foul attempts" to capture them
or use the courts to force them back to Canada and expressed dis-
may with the declaration of martial law in Lower Canada that

hampered trading (and smuggling, a major commercial activity along the border since embargo days), declaring it another example of British tyranny! In general they concluded that the *patriotes* were engaged in "just such a cause as our fathers were engaged in, in the war of the revolution and that they are entitled to the same sympathy and assistance from us that our fathers were from theirs."

The excited people crowded into the meetinghouses at Saint Albans and other towns in Vermont read American history more than a little naively, but not without a purpose. Establishing their own versions of the American Revolution and of their forefathers' heroics, in Vermont often more perceived than real, provided a rationalization for their noisy enthusiasm and identification with the *patriote* cause. But the weak intellectual substance of the resolutions resting on a platform of distorted history went largely unrecognized as it was drowned out by the boisterous rhetoric of the past.

In Middlebury enthusiasts attending the public sympathy meeting entered the court house brightly illuminated in front with a transparency of Papineau and Thomas Storrow Brown suspended from the cupola.[26] High spirits and lively demonstrations had already been initiated with Brown's appearance in Middlebury where he advertised in the local newspaper for guns, knapsacks, and cartouch boxes. His ostensible purpose was "a great Wolf hunt." But rumor had it that he planned "to be on the line with a great military force" in a few weeks.[27] The public meeting, which coincided with the conference of *patriote* leaders at which Nelson assumed command, attracted nearly one thousand avid supporters. The receptive audience cheered the two principal speakers of the evening, "General" T. S. Brown and Louis Perrault (who in Montreal had published the *patriote* newspaper the *Vindicator*), two articulate and active exiles. The correspondent of the *Vermont Argus and Free Press* reported: "The enthusiasm which prevailed in the meeting . . . conducted in the greatest good order and decorum . . . was intense and broke forth in thunder several times. . . . [During a] forcible and impressive speech . . . [Brown] was repeatedly cheered . . . and sat down amid acclamations which shook the

building to its centre. . . . Those in attendance manifested their
true-hearted devotion to the causes of popular liberty, and
their strong sympathy for the Canadian Patriotes, by the propriety and sincerity of their conduct. . . . The spirit of freedom still reigns in the hearts of the sons of the Green Mountains." The meeting adjourned with "three-times-three" for
Papineau and Brown and "an escort was formed at the door
of the Court House, which reached nearly to the Vermont
Hotel."[28]

The resolutions passed in sympathy with the *patriotes* indicated the nature of the "spirit of freedom" that pervaded
Vermont communities in the winter of 1837-38. Redolent with
the rhetoric engendered by the American revolutionary experience, they often synthesized or even copied verbatim the ideas
of the American Declaration of Independence. Corollaries to the
main clauses of resolutions, which generally decried the violation of God-given inalienable rights and liberties, variously pro-
tested the destruction of an opposition press in Montreal (the
short-lived *Canadian Patriot* was established by refugees in the
border town of Derby Line, Vermont, soon after suppression of
the Montreal *Vindicator*); the imposition of martial law in the
province; the killing of Americans at Schlosser, New York, on
the Niagara River in late December 1837; and the tyrannical
rule of Lord Gosford.

The meetings also decried the threats, based for the most part
on homegrown rumors, to "hang or destroy certain good citizens of this State," or in other ways breach the neutrality of the
United States. Many Vermonters apparently entertained frightening visions of ruthless imperialist cavalry sweeping across the
border destroying everything in their path. Setting aside the illogic of their protests against a British breach of American neutrality as they met publicly to proclaim support for rebel violations of neutrality and their own intentions to ignore United
States neutrality laws, the parade of imaginary horrors they
conjured was a transparent attempt at self-justification which
reflected insecurity about their own behavior. Without evidence,
the *North Star* of Danville declared Great Britain and her Canadian henchmen "the aggressor" that had "wantonly invaded our

territory and murdered our citizens."[29] When the "caitiff" of
the *Montreal Herald* threatened the philo*patriote* editor of the
Burlington Free Press, Henry Stacy, with the "noose," even
Stacy could enjoy the notoriety and respond with a jest.[30]
But the thronged meeting at Saint Albans treated the threat as
a pretext to rant about the "arbitrary and bloodthirsty character
of transatlantic toryism which is now flushed with the hope of
reducing the province [Lower Canada] to military despotism."
To combat the international menace they resolved to organize
"a volunteer company to act in defense of our national rights"
and to "recommend to the corps of riflemen and sharp shooters
to clean their rifles, run their balls, supply themselves with powder and be ready at all times to redress any national insult."[31]

The Vermonters became equally indignant when Canadian
border officials and bands of loyalist volunteers patrolled the
line in order "to detect the illegal importation of articles" into
their province.[32] Reacting to the vocal threats from across the
border, Canadians reversed their attitude toward smuggling from
the days when only American officers had tried to prevent illegal
trade during the time of the Embargo and the War of 1812. A
frustrated Canadian officer at East Sherrington reported that
"it would be nearly impossible for him fully to state to His [sic]
Majesty's Government, the great traffic and contraband goods
of every discription [sic], which of late has taken place between
this part of Canada and the United States."[33]

Vermonters who eagerly supplied enough incendiary statements to lend some credence to the Canadian fears were nonetheless upset when movement across the border became more
difficult. In Burlington the *Free Press* announced that "Philo
Weeks is an accredited agent for the Patriot Cause in Lower
Canada, and that he will thankfully receive at Lyman's Hotel
any donation that any person may think proper to bestow,
in order to forward the *Sacred Cause of Liberty*."[34] Three weeks
later, however, the *Free Press* complained "that most or all of
the roads on the line are guarded by loyal militia and that every
person who passes is closely scrutinized. Several persons have
been refused permission to cross the line with their property;
and some have come without it."[35] The Vermonters talked

loosely of using force to end British dominion in Lower Canada while at the same time they demanded that the Canadians open their frontiers for the attempt. When M. Stonehaus of Highgate went to Montreal and was jailed on false charges for twenty-four hours and released when the facts came to the "knowledge of Sir John Colborn [sic]," the *Free Press* determined it to be the underhanded work "of an offended sprig of royalty," a "loyal pimp."[36] Despite the virulence of their rhetoric, the evidence suggests that in reality many Vermonters were concerned lest their public commotion interrupt the regular channels of commerce with Lower Canada. Had they really believed in their own threats, in the last analysis not even these ardent and vocal Vermont democrats could have realistically expected Canadians to sit by and idly countenance an invasion from the south with a shrug of the shoulders and a business-as-usual attitude.

The Canadian loyalists not only allowed the volume of the uproar in Vermont to exaggerate their estimates of the support Americans proposed to give the *patriotes*, but also permitted it to cloud their estimate of the socioeconomic makeup of the philo*patriotes*. It was the contention of the Quebec *Mercury* and of most Canadians, one no less distinguished than Governor Gosford, that the support came from "the lower classes of the inhabitants of the State of Vermont," from shiftless adventurers, unemployed, footloose laborers, and "sojourners in taverns," from men who had little stake in maintenance of the society.[37]

Quite to the contrary, however, the organizers and leaders of the philo*patriote* meetings in Vermont generally consisted of distinguished men in commerce, government, medicine, and the law. The Honorable James Fisk, a justice of the peace and former congressman, local justices of the peace V. S. Ferris and Heman Hopkins, and Dr. J. B. Silly (or Cilly) led the meeting at Swanton on January 5, 1838.[38] The great meeting at Saint Albans on December 19, 1837, drew its leaders from distinguished representatives of the largest towns in Franklin County, including the assistant justice of the Franklin Court, Austin Fuller, who also held the job of postmaster at Enosburg. Others assuming important roles at the Saint Albans meeting were Dr. J. S. Webster of Berkshire, Horace Eaton, an at-

torney from Enosburg, Timothy Foster, a justice of the peace
from Swanton, and Henry Adams, a local lawyer.[39] At Burlington, Guy Catlin, a leading merchant and manufacturer,
Henry B. Stacy, editor of the *Free Press*, and attorney Charles
B. Kasson led the meeting held on December 10, 1837.[40] So
prominent a role did the Catlin family play in supporting the
patriotes that Vermont Governor Silas Jenison directed a letter
to Alec Catlin requesting information for Captain Perkins of
the Stowe Artillery Company of the Vermont Militia "respect-
ing their cannon," which was probably captured by loyalists
when a party of Canadians and their American supporters at
Highgate Springs attempted a raid into Canada. Governor Jenison ordered Catlin to "have the cannon found and restored
to the [Company]. You [Catlin] probably know where the
gun is and I wish you to inform me of that fact by return mail.
The *patriotes* will not probably have any further use for the
gun unless we should have a war with Great Britain."[41] Surviving Catlin papers reveal that Alec loaned money and pro-
visions to a number of destitute refugees, and one letter from
patriote leader Robert Nelson suggests that Catlin helped
raise a large part of the rebel war chest.[42]

In their desperation the *patriotes* also looked beyond their
local champions for aid, frequently allowing their hopes to
elevate rumor to fact, imagination to reality. There was loose
talk of aid from French officers come to help their former
countrymen.[43] The *patriotes* also thought that some help
might be expected from Russia. When in New York City,
Robert Nelson was rumored to have conferred with the "Rus-
sian Consul, who promised him assistance,—that the Imperial
Government of Russia would seize with pleasure this occasion
to avenge in Canada the deep wounds which the Circassians,
sustained by English money and engineers, had inflicted . . . on
the Muscovite armies."[44] They also thought aid was forth-
coming from the state of Maine, where Governor Kent alleged-
ly hoped that *patriote* forays from Vermont could provoke a
general Anglo-American confrontation and provide Maine the
excuse to close in on the territory then in dispute with New
Brunswick.[45]

The possibility of a serious rupture in Anglo-American relations was more than a *patriote* fantasy. President Van Buren
and others anxious to preserve the fragile equilibrium between
the United States and Great Britain feared the balance might
be upset and, with the rivalry in Texas, provoke a two-front
war. The president ordered General Wool to the Vermont border
to keep the neutrality there, while, in Congress, party hack James
Buchanan offered a neutrality bill that prohibited trade in arms
across land frontiers.

In Vermont on December 13, 1837, three days after the first
general meetings of philo*patriotes* in Burlington, Governor
Silas H. Jenison, under pressure from the federal government
and a group of distinguished men from Burlington who had
petitioned him to demand neutrality, issued a proclamation
enjoining his fellow citizens to respect the "profound peace"
between Great Britain and the United States by not furnishing
to any party arms or munitions or any other aid which could
violate long-accepted principles of neutrality. Governor Jenison
preferred that Vermonters should not "jeopardize the peace of
our country" by interfering in the "intestine broils" of another
country.[46]

The attempts to quiet the border agitation incited the wrath
of the philo*patriotes*. They attributed Van Buren's position to
his "devotion to Southern interest," and "cringing and subser-
vient spirit towards Great Britain." They correctly viewed Buchanan's proposal as an exclusive measure aimed at the supporters of the Canadian rebels and denounced it as a move designed to "secure Great Britain in possession of the Canadas by
prohibiting the sale of arms to Canadian malcontents." Between them Van Buren and Buchanan had "volunteered un-
masked concessions . . . asked for by nobody but the British
ambassador," and thus thrown away "the best card in our hand."[47]
Governor Jenison and the Burlington men who had supported
his proclamation received equally harsh treatment. "Under the
influence of such principles," the *Burlington Free Press* scorn-
fully remarked, "the spirit of seventy-six would have been converted into an iceberg, and we at this day have been colonies."[48]

Though not everyone in Vermont supported the *patriotes*,

only a few raised their voices in harmony with Van Buren and Governor Jenison. Public expression was decidedly one-sided in the face of intolerance with those who disagreed with American support for the rebel cause. Observing the frenetic American behavior as he travelled from Montreal to Saint Albans in late 1837, Captain Marryat found it "strange how easily the American people are excited, and when excited, . . . will hesitate at nothing."[49]

The level of public interest and excitement in the *patriote* uprising in Vermont during the winter of 1837-38 was extraordinary. Not even the Embargo or the War of 1812 with their direct threats and political antipathies had caused such an unprecedented series of public meetings. The rebellion in Lower Canada inspired an intense but short-lived emotional cartharsis, which Marryat and other observers misinterpreted by concluding that the Vermonters would follow their rhetoric with deeds. Though the *patriotes* continued to press for their cause until the disastrous defeat they suffered at the final rising in November 1838, and though much of the Canadian-United States frontier remained in turmoil until well into 1842, Vermont interest had generally flagged by the summer of 1838, dying almost as quickly as it had risen. The philo*patriotes* in Vermont were not revolutionaries. The feverish, almost frantic, tone of the great public clamor espousing the spirit of liberty and democratic ideals, almost as if they had personally discovered them, suggests that these Vermonters had more interest in reassuring themselves of who they were than in bestowing their blessings on Canadians.

NOTES

1. Many of the leaders of the *patriotes* had connections with the United States beyond the fact of their exile after the rebellions failed. Dr. Cyrile Coté received his medical degree from the University of Vermont in 1832. Robert Nelson received honorary M.A. degrees from Vermont and Dartmouth in 1831 and held an appointment at the University of Vermont Medical College, which later granted him an honorary degree. See Eugene P. Link, "Vermont Physicians and the Canadian Rebellion of 1837," *Vermont History*, 37 (1969), 178-79. T. S. Brown grew up in Middlebury, and

Dr. E. B. O'Callaghan practised medicine in Albany from 1837 to 1841, thereafter devoting full time to editing documents in New York history, including eleven volumes in the series entitled *Documents Relating to Colonial History of the State of New York* (Albany, 1853-61).

2. The first major work on the causes of the 1837 rebellion, the famous *Report* issued by Lord Durham after his missions to the Canadas, found it, in his often quoted phrase, "a struggle not of principles, but of races," precipitated by "the remains of an ancient civilization," possessing "no history and no literature" (C. P. Lucas, ed., *Lord Durham's Report on the Affairs of British North America* [Oxford, 1912], II, 16, 291, and 294). Partially in an attempt to answer Durham's charges, the first nationalist interpretation, F. X. Garneau's classic *History of Canada* (Montreal, 1862), reinforced the role of racial conflict. Other works, such as Alfred D. DeCelles's *Louis-Joseph Papineau* (Toronto, 1910), have echoed Garneau. The most blatantly nationalist (and largely undocumented) treatment, labelling the English Canadians villains who "consideraient le pays et les Canadiens comme un vaste champ d'exploitation et de gain materiel," was Gerard Filteau's *Histore Des Patriotes*, 3 vols. (Montreal, 1938-1942), I, 33.

In great contrast to the nationalists, the work of scholars such as Helen Taft Manning in *The Revolt of French Canada 1800-1835* (New York, 1962) presented a much more balanced political narrative and along with A. R. M. Lower, *Canadians in the Making* (Toronto, 1958), and others pointed out the weakness of monolithically political interpretations. S. D. Clark in *Movements of Political Protest in Canada 1640-1840* (Toronto, 1959) enthusiastically linked Canadian and United States experiences, especially the influence of the frontier. Mason Wade's chapters concerning the events prior to the rebellion in his comprehensive history, *The French Canadians, 1760-1845* (New York, 1955), still remain a sound political synthesis, while at the same time incorporating many social and economic factors. Joseph Schull's popular account, *Rebellion, The Rising in French Canada 1837* (Toronto, 1971) has not replaced the earlier work. A balanced French Canadian point of view is in the prefatory summary by Felix Leclerc in A. Fauteaux's *Patriotes de 1837-38* (Montreal, 1950).

D. G. Creighton in "The Struggle for Financial Control in Lower Canada, 1818-1831," *Canadian Historical Review*, 12 (March 1931), "The Economic Background of the Rebellions of Eighteen Thirty-Seven," *Canadian Journal of Economics and Political Science*, 3 (August 1937), and his classic *The Commercial Empire of the St. Lawrence* (Toronto, 1937), with a jaundiced eye toward the French, developed an economic interpretation that viewed the rebellion as the result of increasing antagonism between "agrarianism and commercialism, between feudal and frontier agriculture and the commercial state" ("Economic Background,"

p. 235) in a period of instability. R. L. Jones, "French Canadian Agriculture in the St. Lawrence Valley, 1815-1850," *Agricultural History*, 16 (July 1942) and Fernand Ouellet and Jean Hamelin, "La Crise Agricole dans le Bas-Canada, 1802-1837," *Canadian Historical Association Annual Report*, 1962, 17-23, discuss the agricultural problems and suggest their role in precipitating events.

Fernand Ouellet, at present the most active student of the rebellions, has viewed them as the products of complex and interrelated social and economic forces. An accepted authority on Papineau (*Louis-Joseph Papineau: A Divided Soul*, Canadian Historical Society Booklet No. II [Ottawa, 1964]), he has raised many important questions and attempted the answers to some of them in his important *Histoire Economique et Sociale du Quebec 1760-1850* (Montreal, 1966). W. H. Parker, "A New Look at Unrest in Lower Canada in the 1830s," *Canadian Historical Review*, 40 (September, 1959), complementing Ouellet's work, pointed out the explosive potential of the pent-up energy in French-Canadian society, led by an oversupply of priests, notaries, lawyers, and physicians, frustrated in their ambitions and thwarted in commercial pursuits.

3. *Vermont Watchman* (Woodstock), January 29, 1838.

4. *Vermont Patriot*, December 27, 1837.

5. "A Look at Gosford and the Tories," *Vermont Mercury*, December 8, 1837.

6. Ibid., December 20, 1837.

7. Captain Frederick Marryat, *Diary in America*, ed. by Jules Zanger (Bloomington, Ind., 1960), 168. Marryat, the popular English novelist, referred specifically to the editor of the Saint Albans *Messenger*.

8. Andrew Bell, *Men and Things in America*, 2nd ed. (Southampton, England, 1862), 114-15. Bell travelled in the United States and Canada in 1838.

9. While the fight at St. Denis raged, *patriotes* had mutilated the body of Lieutenant George "Jock" Weir, who had been taken prisoner the previous night. This unhappy incident and the years of antipathy, as exemplified by the frequent riots between *patriotes* and loyalists in the streets of Montreal before the rebellion, lent a particularly nasty overtone to the affair.

10. PACS., vol. 391, p. 58. From H. Wells, postmaster of Henryville, Lower Canada, December 6, 1837.

11. Communications between imperial forces in Canada and federal troops in Vermont and New York seem to have been cordial and close. General Wool, commander of a small United States Army force, wrote to Lord Colborne on March 3, 1838: "I have the honor to inform you that Doctors Nelson and Cote . . . surrendered themselves to me with all their forces, cannon, small arms, and ammunition." (PAC, Co. 42, vol. 280, enclosure 5 [microfilm]). In writing to the colonial secretary, Lord Glenelg, Colborne refers to intelligence gained from General Wool's aide-de-camp, Captain Smith, and a Mr. Cody, brother of a United States marshal.

12. One of the most interesting and detailed accounts of the activities of the Lower Canadian rebels in the United States is a voluntary deposition given by a state prisoner at the Montreal prison in November 1838, an extract of which is published in translation in *Report of the State Trials Before a General Court Martial Held at Montreal in 1838-9 Exhibiting a Complete History of the Late Rebellion in Lower Canada* (Montreal, 1839), II, app. 13, pp. 548-61. Though the deposition is anonymous and the circumstances surrounding its recording not clear, most major details are corroborated by other documents, thus backing its credibility.

13. Ibid., 548.

14. Ibid., 548-49.

15. PAC, S., vol. 391, p. 5; and *Burlington Free Press*, December 8, 1837, and January 5, 1838.

16. PAC, S., vol. 395, pp. 104-5, *Memorial* of Harvey E. Elkins, March 29, 1838; and PAC RG4, B37, vol. I, pp. 21-24, *Deposition* of Humphrey Faller, who noted that "liquor was offered to all who would take it."

17. *State Trials*, II, p. 549.

18. Ibid., 549 and 557; and Catlin MSS, Wilbur Collection, UVM, Robert Nelson to Alec Catlin, Saint Albans, October 11, 1838, and Charles Bryant to Alec Catlin, January 13, 1839.

19. Ibid., p. 549.

20. *Burlington Free Press*, January 5, 1838.

21. *Burlington Free Press*, January 26, 1838; and Abby M. Hemenway, ed., *Vermont Historical Gazetteer* (Claremont, N.H., 1877), V, 374.

22. Kellogg MSS, VHS collections.

23. Marryat, *Diary in America*, 167.

24. MS letter, James Marsh to David Read, December 21, 1837, photocopy UVM.

25. *Vermont Mercury*, December 20, 1837.

26. "Young Men's Meeting in Middlebury," *Vermont North Star*, January 6, 1838.

27. *CAD*, 206-7, James Marsh to David Read, January 11, 1838.

28. *Danville North Star*, January 6, 1838.

29. Ibid., January 20, 1838.

30. *Burlington Free Press*, January 5, 1838.

31. *Vermont Mercury*, December 22, 1838. The closest thing to a transatlantic menace was reported in the *Burlington Free Press*, February 2, 1838: "Three armed tories came across the line at Highgate last Thursday; what their object was we do not learn."

32. PAC, S., vol. 391, p. 252, *Memorial* from E. T. Stoddart, Preventive Officer, Stanstead, Lower Canada, in which he claims his low pay does not compensate for the risks the job has come to involve.

33. Ibid., vol. 392, p. 18, James Pritchard to Lord Gosford, East Sherington, Lower Canada, November 3, 1837.

34. November 2, 1837.

35. November 28, 1837.

36. January 12, 1838.

37. PAC, Co. 42, vol. 274, p. 136 (microfilm); and *Quebec Mercury*, December 21, 1838. Historians have also generally accepted the view that American support for the *patriotes* came from the lower classes. A leading student of the issue, A. B. Corey, maintains that the noise was made by Americans in general and Vermonters in particular "the greater part of whom belonged to the inarticulate masses," and suggests therefore "the meetings fell into the hands of the more conservative elements of society," which "gave the meetings, as a rule, an atmosphere of respectability" (pp. 29 and 33). Corey does not explain why the "inarticulate, if noisy, masses," as he calls them a second time, elected conservatives as their leaders, or more to the point, why the same conservatives took the initiative in calling and organizing the public meetings in the first place. Corey might be correct in asserting that the leaders "discouraged" any "overt actions," but this does not necessarily mean, as he suggests, that the leaders were more conservative than their fellow townsmen, who, inarticulate and blind, dumbly turned leadership over to their betters. Albert B. Corey, *The Crisis of 1830-1842 in Canadian-American Relations* (New Haven, 1941).

38. *Danville North Star*, January, 1838; and E. P. Walton, ed., *Walton's Vermont Register and Almanac, 1837* (Montpelier, 1837), 125.

39. *Vermont Mercury*, December 29, 1837; and *Walton's Register*, 91, 92, 124, and 125.

40. *Vermont Mercury*, December 29, 1837. A similar pattern existed for meetings at Danville (January 25, 1838), Ludlow (January 19, 1838), and Royalton (January 10, 1838), where justices of the peace, a town clerk, church deacons, selectmen, postmasters, doctors, lawyers, and others made up the leadership. See *Walton's Register, 1837*, 78, 79, 88, 94, 114, and 115; *Danville North Star*, February 1838; and *Vermont Mercury*, January 26, 1838. The socioeconomic composition of the leadership presents a number of interesting features. There is a close occupational similarity between the leaders of the public meetings in Vermont and the *patriote* leadership, which was dominated by doctors, lawyers, notaries (comparable to a justice of the peace in Vermont), and politicians. In many cases those most active in the Vermont meetings, if not local notables themselves, were related to the most prominent figures in the town. The number of federal employees involved is striking.

41. Catlin MSS, O. W. Butler to Alexander Catlin, March 11, 1839, Wilbur Collection, UVM.

42. Ibid., Dr. Robert Nelson to Alexander Catlin, Saint Albans, October 11, 1838; Demaray to Alexander Catlin, Saint Albans, June 29, 1838; and Charles G. Bryant to Alexander Catlin, Saint Albans, January 13, 1839 and Burlington, May 5, 1838.

43. *Burlington Free Press*, March 2, 1838. Ignoring the fact, as did most other British officials, that there had been little contact, spiritual or other-

wise, between France and her former colony on the St. Lawrence since the French Revolution, Lord Gosford thought that French officers had been imported to aid the rebels. See PAC, Co. 42, vol. 274, Gosford to Glenelg, November 6, 1837 (microfilm).

44. *State Trials*, II, 549.
45. Ibid., 549-50.
46. *Burlington Free Press*, December 15, 1837.
47. *Vermont Watchman*, February 12, 1838.
48. December 15, 1837.
49. Marryat, *Diary in America*, 167.

Figure 1. George Perkins Marsh, circa 1840, daguerreotype
Source: Bailey/Howe Library, UVM

Figure 2. James Marsh, circa 1835, oil portrait
Source: Bailey/Howe Library, UVM

Figure 3. Louis Joseph Papineau, circa 1830, lithograph
by R. A. Sproule
Source: Public Archives of Canada, Ottawa, C = 5462

Figure 4. Alonzo Jackman, circa 1860, photograph
Source: William Arba Ellis, ed., *Norwich University
        1819-1911/Her History, Her Graduates, Her
        Roll of Honor,* vol. 2 (Montpelier, Vt., 1911)

Figure 5. Silas Jenison, circa 1840, steel engraving
Source: Bailey/Howe Library, UVM

Figure 6. "Old White Church," First Congregational
      Society, Burlington, Vermont, site of Jedidiah
      Burchard's revival in December, 1835. This
      building was destroyed by fire on June 23, 1839.
Source: Bailey/Howe Library, UVM

Figure 7. George Wyllys Benedict, circa 1850, daguerreotype
Source: Special Collections, Bailey-Howe Library, UVM

Figure 8. Joseph Torrey, circa 1860, photograph
Source: Bailey/Howe Library, UVM

Figure 9. Wolfred Nelson, circa 1850, sketch by
Jean-Joseph Girouard
Source: Public Archives of Canada, Jean-Joseph
Girouard Collection, C = 18438

CHAPTER FIVE

CIVIL REBELLION AND THE NATURE OF MAN

As public frenzy and a noisy sympathy for the *patriotes* grew during December 1837, opposition to American support of the *patriotes*' cause also began to form in Vermont. The authors of the strongest calls for American neutrality and the sharpest critics of the philo*patriotes*' actions spoke from Burlington. The major statement of the anti*patriotes* was initiated by George Wyllys Benedict of the University of Vermont's faculty and written by the lawyer George Perkins Marsh, who presented a petition to Governor Jenison on December 12, 1837, and then reprinted it in the *Vermont Chronicle* on December 20. Twenty-three leading citizens, including Benedict, the brothers George Perkins and Joseph Marsh, their cousin Professor James Marsh, and his colleagues on the faculty, Farrand Benedict, Joseph Torrey, and John Wheeler, the university's president, requested Governor Jenison to issue a proclamation which would restrict illegal recruiting, arming, and drilling of volunteers to fight with the *patriotes*. The petitioners declared it foolhardy to arouse those harsh feelings between America and England which had lain dormant since the end of the War of 1812. Then, striking a curious note for men with little commercial interest in either Vermont or Canada, they pointed out that commerce with

Canada was too important to be hazarded by war. Moreover, interference with Canadian affairs had no justification, they asserted; and all right-principled men would remain aloof from the quarrels of Canadians with their government. A final important point, around which much of the debate over supporting the *patriotes* would revolve, urged Americans not to "dignify every case of resistance to an established government with the name of liberty . . . though it may often be generous, it is not always just to adopt the quarrel of the weaker party." The petition that George Perkins Marsh and his associates presented, and the governor's proclamation it inspired, brought down on them hostile blasts and "almost universal censure and condemnation" from the press.

Their petition to Governor Jenison rested on, so the petitioners claimed, the practices of political expediency and principles of moral philosophy. The book from which the arguments of the anti*patriotes* drew their substance was one of the most influential texts in nineteenth-century British political liberalism, Samuel Taylor Coleridge's *The Friend: A Series of Essays, to Aid in the Formation of Fixed Principles in Politics, Morals and Religion*, which Professor James Marsh, the first in a long line of American students and commentators on Coleridge, had republished in 1831 with his own introduction through the Burlington publishing firm of his brother-in-law, Chauncey Goodrich.[1]

In the meantime, Professor Marsh began writing a series of twenty lengthy letters to his brother-in-law, David Read, an able lawyer then in Saint Albans at the center of the *patriote* uproar. Though they shared some basically similar assumptions about the nature of man, they justified their divergent views by what they first believed were sharply opposing concepts of the political and social nature of America.[2] Knowing that Read was a prominent figure among the Saint Albans supporters of the Canadian rebels, Marsh, perhaps to defend himself and the other petitioners in Burlington, thought the situation "of moment enough to write." Marsh also hoped the letters would be published in Saint Albans and help restore order. "If you think it can do good," he instructed Read, "publish this in your paper

saying that it was written to an individual in your village sub-
stituting 'sir' for 'brother' in the address." The letters never appeared in the newspaper. But, before Marsh finally told Read
to go and study Coleridge if he would understand the petitioners' arguments, he went to great lengths on his own to explain
the anti*patriote* position.

Marsh's first letter sketched the main points of the anti-
patriotes' argument (12/12/1837). First, Marsh pointed out
that Lower Canada's location along Vermont's northern border
was not sufficient reason to promote revolution there. The question of distance or proximity had no relevance. Instead it should
be asked whether the *patriotes'* cause was a good one or not;
and how could one identify a good cause? If Americans refused
even to ask, much less seek answers to such basic questions,
then interference in Canadian internal affairs was immoral because only opportunistic. They should, instead, stand aloof.

But even settling questions for the good, Marsh went on, left
serious practical questions. For example, did the French Canadians have the capacity for self-government? If their rebellion
succeeded, would they establish a stable society, or would a
native Canadian despotism or, even worse, anarchy replace the
present British rulers? Failure to ask the moral and the practical
questions while still supporting the *patriotes*, Marsh believed,
signified either or both of two serious faults—fanatical hallucina-
tions or reckless ambitions. The former resulted from a blind
pursuit of a political abstract, ideal liberty; the latter derived
from simple greed expressed in the quest for "a little pay and
plunder"[3] or the broader drive toward continental expansion.

For himself Marsh thought that Lower Canadian rebels had
very little chance of success. So, on the purely practical level,
to encourage them would only exacerbate their ultimate failure.
At the same time, he believed that American self-interest could
not be served by a successful rebellion, for "the more peaceful
and prosperous they are among themselves and the more quiet
and orderly in their intercourse, the better it will be for us. Now
what considerate man would wish so far as our interest in this
respect is concerned, to run the hazard of a change from what

we have hitherto experienced," he asked Read, especially if a successful rebellion had no certainty of bringing the kind of government that would sustain the peaceful and orderly exchanges with Canada that the United States enjoyed.

Despite the logical development of his reasoning and its suggestion of aloof, intellectual objectivity, Marsh, in his own way, had an emotional investment in opposition to the *patriotes* that paralleled Read's enthusiasm for them. He dismissed "the Canadians as a people . . . utterly incapable of self-government," and the entire affair as "either the blind hallucination of fanaticism or the wicked and reckless ambition of a few leaders to blow the trumpet of political liberty and talk of our glorious revolution to the great mass of Canadian French nine tenths of whom can neither read nor write, who certainly have no strength of religious or even moral principle and whose very leaders . . . [have] given no such proofs of serious and well grounded principles." Then, with a sideways glance at Jackson's Democrats, Marsh suggested that his own reactions to the *patriote* uprising in part provided an outlet for other frustrations. It did not "become us," he declared, "to talk of the British government as one among the European despotisms when we all know that our government for the last eight years has been more despotic and inflicted more wanton evil upon its subjects than any British sovereign could have done for many a year without losing his throne or his life" (12/12/1837).[4]

Then, in this opening installment of a debate carried on until after the most intense excitement over the *Patriote* War had subsided in Vermont, Marsh, perhaps unwittingly, revealed the basis of his personal opposition to the philo*patriotes*, though he couched it in the rhetoric of moral and philosophical arguments. Because the strain of living in a growing democracy was difficult and testing, he hoped that "we may prove capable of shunning its *extreme* dangers," such as the constant threat of a demagogue rising to power. Though in his view party factionalism constantly threatened to divide the country and the extremes of anarchy or tyranny always lurked below the surface of American life, he could still see no reason to reject democracy. Rather, self-government should be seen as a promising but ambiguous political system under which people can thrive, but uneasily and with difficulty. Yet Americans should take care not to export it heedlessly. Especially, he warned Read, if the people to whom it is exported have been good neighbors, Americans should not force on them something so tenuous and difficult to sustain as democracy. Should democratic self-government fail in Canada, despite support of the *patriotes*, Americans would cry for annexation as a means of stabilizing relations with their northern neighbor. Continental expansion of that sort, Marsh asserted, could be nothing more than a thin disguise for greed. Thus the ideal of political liberty would be sacrificed on the altar of materialism.

Knowing that he might appear dangerously close to "becoming zealous . . . against zealotry" and "very anti-popular," Marsh nonetheless continued his criticism of the philo*patriotes* and their resolutions, many of which he deemed "very sophomorical." The first interest of the United States, he lectured Read, lay in its own political and economic security. If Canada were well-governed; if its government did not really harm the United States as it went about its day-to-day relations with her; and if the United States found her easy to deal with, all the better. Marsh's political rubric relative to Canadian affairs simply said: support no change in Canada. *Who* governs Canada he found a "matter of perfect indifference so it be well governed." From the American point of view she enjoyed good government, so why interfere?

This first letter to Read and the following two (12/14/1837 and 12/15/1837) covered the main points of the arguments for nonparticipation in the *Patriote* War; and Marsh regarded his explication of the arguments as quite thorough. The next few letters in the series, however, suggest that while Marsh and his fellow petitioners firmly believed the rightness of their position and knew it ran counter to popular feelings, the vehemence and, in their view, the illogic of the resolutions passed at a meeting of philo*patriotes* held in Saint Albans on December 11th, shocked and surprised them. Marsh and his friends were also very upset by the harsh insults and public castigation they received for having written the petition that stimulated Governor Jenison's proc-

lamation calling for neutrality. In the face of such violent statements Marsh felt compelled to write another letter to Read.[5]

The incident that provoked the Saint Albans resolutions took
place on December 6th when a force of less than one hundred
patriotes and their American supporters marched into Canada
from Swanton, Vermont, only to be greeted at Moore's Corners,
a little village north of the border, by six hundred English regulars
and loyalists waiting in ambush on a ledge overhanging the road.
A battle lasting only twenty minutes cost the *patriotes* two leaders, Robert Bouchette and Julius Gagnon, two thousand rounds
of ammunition, cannon powder, and their cannon recently "liberated" from the Vermont militia company at Stowe.[6] The main
body of the *patriote* force retreated to Swanton where liberty
lovers received them and let it be known that they "despise[d]
the threats of the vile instruments of a Tory government and
will protect at all hazards the Canadian *patriotes* who have fled
to our land of liberty for protection."[7] The resolutions of the
Saint Albans philo*patriotes* rebuked Governor Jenison for failing to protect Vermont and expressed outrage at the injuries
visited upon Vermonters who had taken part in the "invasion."
They also complained about the Canadian declaration of martial
law and restrictions, such as searching, placed on Americans entering the British colony.

Astounded by the irrational outrage he detected in the resolution passed at Saint Albans, Marsh asked Read how Americans
could on the one hand condemn the Canadian government and
incite and aid the rebels, for which some Vermonters took some
bruises, and on the other "complain and commence with charging the authorities of the province with infraction of treaties?"
How, too, could Vermonters be "affected by the proclamation
of martial law in Canada so long as they keep at home and mind
their own concerns?" (12/14/1837).

The Saint Albans's resolutions claimed the absolute right of
Americans to enter Canada. But, Marsh pointed out, any treaty
only conditionally guaranteed alien free entry, and Americans
had no right or authority by the terms of any treaty to judge
when a foreign government could impose martial law on its

citizens and establish conditions of alien entry which required searching luggage or transported goods for contraband.

For Marsh the local Saint Albans resolutions bore directly on the question of freedom of speech when they concerned national relations with Canada and Great Britain. Marsh asked Read to enquire of his neighbors in Saint Albans if, considering all the circumstances of the case, it was decent—practically fair—to pass judgment on another government's actions while legally at peace with it. Was it wise to "applaud those who are in rebellion against it, as only claiming the rights which are inherent in every people?"

The First Amendment guaranteed the right to speak freely only in the United States. Any real threats or violent action taken against Vermonters by Canadians on United States soil, either officially or by other loyalist supporters of British rule in Canada should, of course, have public attention drawn to them. However, Marsh noted, the Canadian militia infringed American liberties only when Americans had seen fit illegally to carry those liberties into Canada. No American martyr for liberty would appear among the philo*patriotes*, Marsh thought, as long as they stayed south of the border with Henry Stacy, the editor of the Burlington *Free Press* who had been threatened by the "waspish" editor of the Montreal *Herald* for publishing inflammatory editorials.[8]

Finally, Marsh responded to those philo*patriotes* in Saint Albans and other Vermont towns who insisted on comparing the Lower Canada uprising to the American Revolution.[9] Had he known of it, Marsh doubtless would have pointed to the irony of *patriote* General Thomas Storrow Brown's United Empire Loyalists heritage to underscore the inept contrast in comparing the *patriote* outburst to the American Revolution. He had other reasons for refusing to make the comparison, however: "My notion of the state of things in Canada and of the population there must be vastly different from what they now are before I should be willing to degrade the American revolution by any sort of comparison of it with these doings. Look at the *occasion*, at the *leading men*, at the *public documents* in which their *grounds of complaint*, their principles of action, their purposes are set forth . . . and see if it is not sinking a great way into pathos to pass from the opening of our revolutionary drums to the opening of the Canada quarrel."

By Christmas 1837 the agitation in Vermont for the *patriotes* diminished a little for a time, perhaps, as Marsh suggested, because of Governor Jenison's proclamation of neutrality. The affair of the steamboat *Caroline* on the Niagara River had not yet occurred and little attention seems to have been directed westward from Vermont. In the next week the Canadian loyalist leader Allan McNab ordered the raid from Upper Canada on the *Caroline*, a steamboat docked at Schlosser, New York, and used to ferry arms and men to the rebels on Navy Island in the Niagara River. Unaware of events on the Niagara frontier, that week Marsh's correspondence with Read indicated that the debate within Vermont had now reached the point at which both parties could begin to construct theoretical and philosophical justifications for their respective positions.

The general proposition which Marsh asserted on December 24th attacked the philo*patriotes* for their "general and vague assertions that every people have the right to choose their own government, to be independent, etc." But that right, according to Marsh, "must be so limited by condition as will make them too narrow for your purpose as applied to the case in hand. . . . In matters of revolutions we must determine *from all the circumstances of each case* by itself whether it is justifiable or not." Marsh and his fellow petitioners, on the other hand, admitted that they had "not the means or the information necessary *thus to determine on this case*," though they did "know enough negatively to justify . . . withholding . . . sympathy and cooperation" (12/24/1837).

Marsh and Read continued their debate into the new year. As the activities of the *patriotes* in Vermont became less public and the focus of the insurgency moved westward to the Niagara frontier, Marsh and Read continued to construct more complete theoretical bases for their own positions on the question of American support for the *patriote* cause. On January 6th Marsh told Read that "in reference to certain more general principles of politics will you read with care Coleridge's Friend from the 140th to the 194th page. If you will consult the principles there taught, I shall be prepared to look at the Canada question by new lights and perhaps come to different conclusions."

The likelihood of Marsh changing his mind about Canadian affairs was not very great, but if he could lure Read into a philosophical debate based on Samuel Taylor Coleridge's political theories, he might win a war of words and justify his own stance. He might even have continued to hope that his letters would find their way into the Saint Albans newspaper and at once help calm the excited populace and defend the Burlington petitioners. Unlike his knowledge of Canada, Marsh's interest in Coleridge was long-standing and thorough. As one of the leading American exponents of the English poet-philosopher's ideas, he introduced them *ex cathedra* in philosophy courses at the University of Vermont.[10]

Marsh had republished *The Friend* in 1831. Perhaps because Coleridge criticized many contemporary democratic practices, *The Friend* met an enthusiastic reception during Jackson's first term among conservatives in places as distant from Vermont as Pittsburgh, Pennsylvania, and Kentucky. In the early thirties, John W. Nevins of Pittsburgh, the future president of Mercerburg Theological Seminary, published a newspaper called *The Friend*, prominently featuring excerpts from and discussions of Coleridge. In Kentucky a New School Presbyterian leader wrote to Marsh thanking him for introducing Coleridge to Americans.[11] Marsh easily equated what he regarded as the licentious behavior of "King Andrew's" Democracy and the unbridled press that supported him, such as Isaac Hill's *New Hampshire Patriot*, with the role of the Vermont press during the *patriote* uprising. Marsh complained to Read that the press was "one of the greatest issues in the land . . . tending more effectively than any thing else to loosen the foundation of all law and government." Unhappily, he concluded, " 'political calumny' has already joined hands with private slander, and every principle, every feeling that binds the citizen to his country and the spirit to its Creator will be undermined" (1/11/1838).

In a time like the early 1830s, when any call for a critical examination of the expanding American democracy would be officially questionable, the very introduction of *The Friend* represented a pure Coleridgean gesture in more senses than one. As Walter Jackson Bate has noted, Coleridge was not himself quick to express unorthodox views publicly.[12] Early in his life Coleridge developed a public role of usher, sympathetically escorting views attributed to someone else. The role released Coleridge's creative energies in his poetry as well as his prose works, operating quite effectively in *The Friend* and *Aids to Reflection*, both of which Marsh republished in America with his own sympathetic introductory commentaries. By referring Read to Coleridge, Marsh acted in a critical role similar to Coleridge.

The main concern of the passages in *The Friend* that Marsh asked Read to study, entitled "On the Principles of Political Philosophy," argued the impracticability of Rousseau's *Du Contrat Social*. To make such a bald assertion to Read, even in light of all his earlier pessimistic predictions about the chances for success in an independent Canada, certainly verged on political heresy. By ushering in Coleridge's essay on the impracticability of *Du Contrat Social* and the failure of French physiocracy in the 1790s, however, Marsh could direct the debate into his own area of greatest learning and argumentative strength, moral philosophy. What Marsh wanted Read to recognize, and thereby accede to the essential rightness of Marsh's arguments and the good sense of the petitioners, was the failure of the physiocrats, like the philo*patriotes*, to account for the role of human failings in their pursuit of the political ideal of universal liberty. Coleridge had asserted that in attempting to derive universal political principles from Reason, followers of Rousseau neglected to recognize that "universal principles, as far as they are principles and universals, necessarily suppose uniform and perfect subjects, which are to be found in the *Ideas* of pure Geometry and (I trust) in the *Realities* of Heaven, but never, never, in creatures of flesh and blood."[13] Read soon realized that Marsh had argued him into a corner, but he made a good try at defending himself and the philo*patriotes*.

"I have looked into the *Friend* and think it rather a hard tax that you have imposed upon me—It is much easier to *adopt* than to *criticize* the arguments of so learned and distinguished a man as Coleridge," he told Marsh on January 8th. He tactfully concluded, from reading the pages Marsh recommended, that Rousseau and Coleridge were "both in the *right* and both in the *wrong*":

> Rousseau was in the *right* as to his abstract principles of Government and Coleridge was in the *right* in contending that the natural imperfections of man unfit him and remained a lasting, at least an existing, obstacle against the enjoyment of those principles. Rousseau was *wrong* in advocating as practicable a form of government which could only be applied to man and enjoyed by him, when divested of his corrupt and sinful nature . . . Coleridge was in the *wrong* in denying the justice of these principles when applied to Government after having so manfully contended for them as applicable to man.

Coleridge, Read believed, erred in attributing to national governments only the power of the 'Understanding', the calculating faculty which Coleridge and German philosophical idealism defined as relying solely on the evidence of the senses, and attributing the power of Reason, a kind of suprasensual or intuitive mode of knowing, to individuals. Read, with characteristic American optimism, looked forward to the day when nations would be governed by Reason. He asked Marsh if "mankind can be brought to that elevation" when political "doctrines which we now call Jacobinical may find in time to come a successful application to a higher and more elevated station of human perfectability?"
Either Read had misread Coleridge, or he realized that Marsh had argued him into a corner and used the interrogatory note of hope for the future to deflect the thrust of Marsh's Coleridgean parry. Actually Coleridge had written that

> From Reason alone can we derive the principles which our Understandings are to apply, the ideal to which by means of our Understandings we should endeavor to approximate.

This however gives no proof that Reason alone ought to
govern and direct human beings, either as individuals or
as States. It ought not to do this, because it cannot.[14]

Sound government, Coleridge claimed, followed the maxim
"*expedience* founded on *experience* and particular circumstances,
which will vary in every different nation, and in the same nation at different times."[15]

Marsh responded on January 11 asking Read if he did not
"see that if you only admit as you do that the abstract principles
of reason cannot be applied absolutely but must be modified by
the character and condition of the particular people, you have
in fact granted all that is necessary in reference to the case before" (1/11/1838).

The central philosophical point of the debate between Marsh
and Read had been won, whether Read understood it or not.
By allowing himself to argue on Marsh's terms in the arena of
moral philosophy and then admitting the basic validity of Marsh's
arguments from the imperfection of human nature, Read left
the field clear for those who argued against the wisdom and
propriety of supporting the *patriotes* to win the debate. Moreover, when Read first admitted the proposition of human imperfection and then expressed a hope for a future state of perfection in which Reason could operate, he wrote about achieving
the goals of an education in which at least six of the twenty-three
petitioners had a professional interest and competency and at
least one other, George Perkins Marsh, exercised a keen layman's
interest.

In 1829 the faculty of the University of Vermont redesigned
the curriculum with the same goals Read's note of hope suggested in 1838 and according to the Coleridgean distinction between Reason and Understanding.[16] In 1837-38, the same curriculum still functioned according to that design. Coleridgean
modifications of German philosophical idealism shaped the
senior-year philosophy course in an effort to prepare citizens
who, according to an address delivered by James Marsh in
1830, would not leave academic life for the larger Vermont

and American communities with only an eager and unreflect-
ing "pursuit of worldly interest and ambition," but would
instead be equipped to make the "careful and thorough examination [to justify revolutions, for instance] . . . by the
light of past experience, by the exercise of that sound and
deep political wisdom which few possess" and which, he told
Read in 1838, never manifested itself at philo*patriote* meetings.[17]

It would have been difficult for Read to answer Marsh after
that; and no extant letters from Read indicate that he ever
tried. Marsh had taken Read into the anti*patriote* camp and
disarmed him. Finally, Marsh begged Read's pardon for the
harsh tone of some of his earlier letters and the debate between these two articulate and intelligent spokesmen for the
anti- and philo*patriotes* broke off.

In the meantime, much of the verbal excitement over the
Patriote War had passed from Vermont since the early part of
January. The *Caroline* affair on December 29th and the activities
of Federal troops under General Winfield Scott on the Niagara
frontier drew the public's attention, and though Marsh and Read
briefly disputed the propriety of the philo*patriotes* activities
in western New York in some of their letters in early and mid-
January, the heat of debate in Vermont over the *Patriotes'*
uprising cooled and the public's interest in Canadian affairs
gradually diminished during the winter of 1838. Marsh had
suggested to Read early in their debate that in six months
prominent citizens of Vermont among the philo*patriotes* would
finally realize "the mock-heroic and ridiculous character" of
their behavior. Six months and then some passed before the
final episode of the *Patriote* War took place in Vermont.

In November 1838 Robert Nelson led three thousand American and Canadian followers on a "Wolf hunt" into Lower Canada
near Napierville in the Richelieu River Valley. An army of Loyalists and British regulars soon routed Nelson's ragged force and
twelve of the captured "hunters" were eventually executed for
treason. Marsh, however, did not live to see the ultimate resolution of his debate with Read and enjoy the irony of its classical

comedy ending. He died in 1842, some ten years before his niece, Caroline Pitkin, married Louis-Joseph Papineau, grandson of the *patriote* leader.

NOTES

1. Samuel Taylor Coleridge, *The Friend: A Series of Essays, To Aid in the Formation of Fixed Principles in Politics, Morals, and Religion, with Literary Amusements Interspersed.* 1st American ed., 1 vol. (Burlington, Vt., 1831).

2. The correspondence between Marsh and Read is contained in *CAD* and as MSS in the Wilbur Collection, UVM. They are cited parenthetically by date in this chapter.

3. Andrew Bell, *Men and Things in America* (Southampton, 1862), 115.

4. Despite the harshness of his argument and the intemperance of some of the language, Marsh closed the letter to his brother-in-law "with love to all yours very truly" and thanked him for kindness to his son.

5. The *Vermont Mercury*, December 29, 1837, printed the resolution adopted at the Saint Albans meeting. The first comments on the petition to Governor Jenison, which Marsh had helped his cousin George to draft, appeared in the *Burlington Free Press*, December 15, 1837: "The petition of our townsmen to the Governor, should have been addressed to 'Her youthful majesty the Queen,' for surely never were more loyal or royal sentiments offered at the foot of the throne." Attacks in the newspaper of "Lord Gosford's twenty-three most Loyal subjects in Burlington," increased after the first of the new year; *see Danville North Star*, January 8, 1838, and *Vermont Mercury*, January 10, 1838. The latter reported a meeting at Royalton where philo*patriotes* resolved "that we view with perfect execration and abhorrence the conduct of certain wise ones in Burlington, in petitioning the governor of this state to send forth their (not his) proclamation forbidding our charities . . . or our sympathies in behalf of the suffering Canadians."

6. *Burlington Free Press,* December 8, 1837.

7. *Vermont Mercury,* December 22, 1837.

8. The *Burlington Free Press*, January 5, 1838, reprinted a paragraph from the *New Hampshire News:* "We perceive . . . that the editor of the Burlington *Free Press* has been threatened by the caitiff of the Montreal *Herald* with a *noose.* Our brethren of the press at Burlington will confer a favor by informing us in this section, when this *noose game* is to take place as most of our people would like to be present." Henry Stacy, editor of the *Free Press*, responded: "Now as it is not probable that we shall go to Canada at present, if this royal volunteer [the *Herald*'s editor] will fix a day certain when he will attend to the duties of his appointment at this

place, we will endeavor to be at home, and with his permission, invite a few friends to witness a public demonstration of the 'mild and paternal character of Her Majesty's government.' "

9. "The Democratic Platform," a weekly column in the *Danville North Star*.

10. *CAD*, 233, James Marsh to Henry Nelson Coleridge, July 16, 1840.

11. On Nevins's newspaper, *The Friend, see* John Hastings Nichols, *Romanticism in American Theology* (Chicago, 1961), 57, and *CAD*, 122-24, 168-69, letter from Thomas P. Smith to James Marsh, January 27, 1832, and November 14, 1834. Smith was known as "Mr. Presbyterian" in Kentucky.

12. Walter Jackson Bate, *Coleridge* (New York, 1968), 131-38.

13. Coleridge, *The Friend*, 173.

14. Ibid., 170.

15. Ibid., 173.

16. Julian Lindsay, *Tradition Looks Forward/The University of Vermont* (Burlington, 1954), 135-49.

17. "Necessary Agency of Religious Truth in the Cultivation of the Mind. [Delivered at the Dedication of the Chapel of the University of Vermont, 1830]." *The Remains of the Rev. James Marsh* . . . , ed. by Joseph Torrey (Boston, 1843), 593.

CHAPTER SIX

VERMONTERS HEROIC AND OTHERWISE

Understanding the actions of Vermonters either attracted to or repelled by the New Measure revivals and the *Patriote* War requires the examination in some detail of the movements of groups of men in society. And, too, the flow of ideas and the rhetoric informing such ideas affect both the lives of individuals and the directions of society. But what can specifically be said about some of the individual actors in this story? What do events in their lives show us of America and Vermont in the 1830s?

Some Vermonters afford us access to certain textures of life in their time and place. Prominent figures in the cultural and intellectual life of Vermont, James Marsh or his cousin George Perkins Marsh, for example, have already appeared in this study. Others, such as Silas Jenison, governor of Vermont during the *Patriote* War, played an important role in shaping events and their outcomes. Some Vermonters seem to have been only models of patriotic behavior and were themselves apparently not directly affected by either the revivals or the excitement caused by the events in Canada and on the border. Still others threw themselves into the midst of the response to the Canadian affair, either in an effort to maintain neutrality or in attempts forcefully to aid the Canadian rebels. And some men seem to have been drawn to the event by the power of the rhetoric of the era.

James and George Perkins Marsh were first cousins, grand-
sons of Joseph Marsh, on whose farm in Hartford, Vermont,
James was born.[1] Joseph Marsh had been Vermont's first
lieutenant governor and had fought in the Revolution at the
Battle of Bennington with his sons Charles and Daniel, fathers
of George and James. Joseph was also among the leaders of a
movement in the late 1770s to establish a separate state con-
sisting of towns on the east and west banks of the Connecticut
River in both New Hampshire and Vermont. Radical frontiers-
men from towns west of the Green Mountains range, however,
objected to the Marshes' and their friends' efforts and their
aristocratic attitudes. Ethan Allen, no friend to real aristocrats
from New York in the west or pretensions thereto east of the
mountains in the recently declared state of New Connecticut,
called the Marshes and their party "A Petulant, Pettifogging,
Scribling sort of Gentry, that will keep any Government in
hot water till they are thoroughly brought under [control] by
the Exertion of Authority." George (1801-1882) and James
(1794-1842), then, were children of putative "founding fathers."[2]

The Marsh cousins were at Dartmouth during and shortly after
the troubled times of the Dartmouth College Case.[3] The college
from 1816 to 1820, as all of her alumni and some legal historians
recall from Daniel Webster's plea before Chief Justice Marshall,
was indeed a small college. Only 157 degrees were awarded in
that time. Nearly half of these graduates became clergymen, for,
like other early American colleges, Dartmouth had deep religious
roots. It was perhaps inevitable, then, that the beginning of the
controversy which resulted in the Dartmouth College Case and
Webster's tear-compelling plea to John Marshall and the United
States Supreme Court for his small, beloved college would have
religious as well as political and personal sources.

The whole affair began in 1804 when Roswell Shurtleff was
appointed professor of divinity and pastor of Hanover Congregational Church against the wishes of President John Wheelock,
son of Dartmouth's founder, Eleazer Wheelock. Shurtleff fostered
the revivalist tradition at Dartmouth during the Second Great
Awakening: during one month in 1815, 120 students and towns-
folk, including James Marsh and Lucia Wheelock, John's niece,

were formally accepted into the church after conversions compelled by Shurtleff's sermons on such texts as "the harvest is past, the summer is ended." James and Lucia, a surviving letter suggests, approached the altar together on the day of their conversions, just as they would again nine years later when they married.[4]

By 1817, while both James and George attended the college, the dispute between then ex-President Wheelock and the board of trustees of the college over Shurtleff's appointment had developed into a personal and political dispute which resulted in the legislature of New Hampshire establishing a rival university and prohibiting the college's faculty and students from entering or using the buildings in Hanover. Some of the students, including the Marshes, were able to resist the distractions of intra- and extramural conflict by regularly meeting in a small discussion group or literary club which had formed in 1813-14, James's first year at Dartmouth. James would proceed bachelor of arts in August 1817; George in 1820.[5]

In 1818, after a year at Andover Theological Seminary, James returned to Dartmouth as a tutor, remaining there until 1820. It was a period in which both men worked vigorously to become polylingual, further improving previously learned Greek, Latin, and Hebrew, while adding French, Spanish, Italian, Portuguese, and German to their repertoire. In these years George developed his first interest in Scandinavian literature.[6]

James returned to Andover in 1820 to complete his theological studies and George went back across the Connecticut River to Norwich where Colonel Alden Partridge hired him as professor of Greek and Latin for his American Literary, Scientific, and Military Academy, the name of which would later be changed to Norwich University. But George found the students boorish and after one year returned to his home in Woodstock to read law with his father. Because of his weakened eyesight, however, other members of the family had to read to him. James, in the meantime, completed his ministerial studies at Andover and in 1822 wrote a lengthy review-article for the *North American Review* entitled "Ancient and Modern Poetry." George Ticknor, who arranged for Marsh to appear in the Boston magazine, considered his essay one of the best to appear in the *Review*. The editor, Edward Everett, thought that Ticknor wrote the review, "as he did not suppose any one who had not been to Europe could know any thing of the subject of it."[7] Marsh's essay clearly demonstrated how extensively he had read during and since his years at Dartmouth. He drew on a wide variety of sources in historical scholarship. His reliance on the German scholars, Grimm, Eichhorn, Schlegel, and Mendelsohn indicated a close familiarity with the most important schools of cultural history in Europe at the time. In addition, his reading in contemporary literature, including Byron, Wordsworth, Coleridge, and Madame de Staël, as well as his knowledge of medieval love poetry, Dante, the *gestes* of Charlemagne, and, of course, the works of the early church fathers and classical Greek and Roman writers, all indicated a familiarity with ancient and modern literature almost amazing for a young man who had studied only at a very rustic Dartmouth and the conservative seminary at Andover.

Unable to find employment at Yale or Princeton, however, James in 1823 finally went to Virginia with John Holt Rice, founder of the Union Theological Seminary in Richmond. After three years in Virginia at Hampden-Sydney College, a period interrupted by a journey north to marry Lucia at Hanover in 1824, James was called back to Vermont as president of the University of Vermont in 1826, one year after George had established his practice in Burlington.

Burlington as it approached 1830 was a busy little town on the east shore of Lake Champlain. With a good harbor it provided easy connections to New York City and other points south by sail or steam "uplake" to the new canal leading to the Hudson River. "Downlake" led to Canada and the northern markets of Saint John, Montreal, and Quebec. Burlington served Chittenden County, when the population had nearly reached 21,000, with sixteen English and West Indies dry goods stores overlooking the harbor, seven blacksmiths, six taverns, four tailors, five joiners, three masons, two barbers, two watchmakers and jewelers, two banks, two meetinghouses, a courthouse and stone jail, and seventeen attorneys. The university enrolled about sixty undergraduates and forty medical students.[8]

In late 1825 George had entered legal practice in Burlington
as the partner of B. F. Bailey. The contrast at first must have
been obvious, according to David Lowenthal: at twenty-nine
Ben Bailey was popular, handsome, and already a successful
civil lawyer; George Marsh, at twenty-four, was serious, attenta-
tive to detail, heavy of build, and weak-eyed. He did most of the
office work; but his skills were soon recognized and he was
chosen a Burlington selectman in 1831-32. George married the
daughter of a prosperous merchant. Cousin James, soon
after his inauguration in Montpelier, settled into Burlington
with Lucia, intending to carry out his plans for revising the
college's curriculum, a proposal for which he presented to
the board of corporators at their first meeting of his presidency,
March 25, 1827. James's revised curriculum proposed to allow
the admission of part time students who were required also to
work at supporting themselves and thus could not attend college full time; elective courses were to be available; and students
were to be allowed to progress through the course of study as
their ability permitted rather than being compulsorily grouped
with no attention to the learning they might accomplish. A
year later James reported to the board of corporators that he
was moderately satisfied with the results of the new curriculum
but felt it suffered mostly from the lack of good textbooks.[9]
    Physically the cousins differed considerably. James was tall,
thin, gentle of manner, weak of voice. He was uncomfortable—
because ineffective in speech, he thought—whenever he had
to address an audience in church or college lecture hall. His
strength as an educator seems to have been in the personal
guidance he gave as an advisor and in the idea of an education
he realized in the curriculum of the university. Weakened by
tuberculosis as early as 1820, during the thirties James's strength
declined, as did his control of the university and his efforts to
bring to publication his essays and notes in logic and metaphysics.
His first wife, Lucia, died of tuberculosis in 1828. In 1829-33
he saw the bulk of his writing appear in print—translations, articles
on popular education, his editions and introductions to Coleridge's *Aids to Reflection* and *The Friend*, and a lengthy article
in the *Christian Spectator*. His two-volume translation of Her-

der's *Spirit of Hebrew Poetry* was published in 1833. In 1830
he married Laura, Lucia's sister, and his in-laws came to live
with him and his new wife and two sons. But only eight years
later, Laura would also die of tuberculosis. James himself suc-
cumbed to the same disease in 1842.

George Perkins Marsh, by contrast with his cousin James, was
physically robust, except for recurring difficulties with his eyesight. He was, too, as his biographer observed, full of Yankee in-
genuity and the ability to do well a dozen things at once.[10] Between leaving Dartmouth in 1820 and his election to Congress in
1842, he engaged in lumbering, farming, manufacturing, school
teaching, and editing a newspaper (Burlington's *Northern Sentinel*);
he engaged in state politics, practiced law, built roads, quarried
marble, made tools, and designed buildings. His design for the
Washington Monument in later years was final and now is familiar
to all visitors to the District of Columbia. He worked and was
reasonably successful at so many enterprises that he once complained in a letter that his "father made a mistake in turning me
out an indifferent lawyer instead of a really good mechanic."
George Perkins Marsh, in David Lowenthal's opinion, epitomized
Emerson's American Scholar: a man eager for action, to whom
"Drudgery, calamity, exasperation, . . . [and] want . . . [were]
instructors in Wisdom and eloquence."[11]

But frustrations and disappointments, even personal disaster,
came to both of the Marshes during their years in Burlington.
George's first disappointment came when, as editor of the *Northern Sentinel*, he joined Ben Bailey and former Governor Cornelius
Van Ness in support of Andrew Jackson. Thinking that Jackson
opposed a tariff on their wool, the majority of Vermont's voters
in 1828 cast their vote for Adams, and Marsh's first political
career ended. Then, in 1833, his first wife, Harriet Buell, died of
heart failure, only to be followed nine days later by their son
Charles who died from complications following scarlet fever. A
substantial cash and property inheritance from Harriet and her
father, Colonel Ozias Buell, improved Marsh's financial position
in the mid-1830s and allowed him to attempt projects like a road
to the Winooski River Falls and the construction of a woolen mill

powered by the river, though fire and flood both damaged the
mill. His law practice would have remained of a sufficient size
to require his attention into the late 1830s, but he found his
clients for the most part socially, if not morally, offensive; and
so he gave less attention to his legal practice each year.

Then, in 1835, George ran as a Whig for Vermont's Supreme
Legislative Council, the upper chamber of the General Assembly
until the Constitutional Convention abolished the council and
provided for a senate in 1836. Running on an Anti-Mason and
Whig coalition slate, Marsh won with one to two thousand more
votes than the rest of the coalition's candidates. But in the meantime the popular election for Governor was undecided and thrown
into the Joint Assembly. After sixty-three ballots of the assembly
failed to provide a majority for William Palmer, despite his plurality in the popular vote, Marsh, as chairman of the judiciary committee, decided that the Constitution of Vermont permitted the
lieutenant governor to become governor by legislative appointment. Silas Jenison of Shoreham served as acting governor by
legislative appointment until he was elected by popular vote in
1836. Marsh's role in moving Jenison into the governorship
would serve him well when he carried the petition of Vermont's
anti*patriotes* to the then-elected Governor Jenison in 1838 and
successfully requested the governor to proclaim Vermont's
neutrality in the Canadian affair and assure that the state's militia
would act to enforce that neutrality if necessary.

But Marsh's growing reputation for public persuasion, an
ability never acquired by his cousin James, brought about his
next political defeat. The only significant item on the legislative agenda after solving the governorship problem was legisla-
tion to reform the debtors laws. In 1830 and again in 1834
George Perkins Marsh had been a loud voice in Vermont for reforming these laws and his efforts helped bring about the exemp-
tion of household goods from seizure and the establishment of
the laws allowing debtors freedom after surrendering property.
The issue of imprisonment for debt was major, for the debtors
laws in the early 1830s sent four thousand Vermonters to jail;
and thus more than 1.5 percent of the state's population knew

this humiliating experience during the first years of the decade.[12] In an economy with little cash money changing hands, credit was an important element in the lives of all Vermonters. For example, as president of the University of Vermont, James Marsh earned a salary of $700 annually. In 1828, the University's ledgers show, he received less than $100 cash, having charged all of his expenses, over $600, to the university's accounts with Burlington merchants.

Burlington stood strongly for abolition of imprisonment for debt, and understandably so since, in one period of nine months in the early thirties, 487 people went to jail for debt while thirteen were imprisoned for other crimes. But in 1835 George Marsh thought the new bill proposing total abolition of imprisonment for debt went too far and thus failed to consider the rights of the lender. He persuaded the council not to concur with the House, and the reform bill died. Popular reaction was so great, however, that six days after the assembly adjourned, Vermont's Constitutional Convention abolished the council in favor of a senate by a two-to-one vote. George Perkins Marsh had effectively talked himself out of a job.

Despite George's political defeat, however, the Marshes' skills in language continued to hold their attention and demand their energies through the following years. An important feature of James's life in the 1830s was the small group discussions he held in his home for his students. They appear to have been such popular events that Richard Henry Dana, Jr., just back from his two years before the mast, tried to join his brother in one of these small groups, only to find Marsh had no more room.[13] But, as his strength would allow, James also gave his time and thought to learning and scholarship in language and logic.[14] George, too, continued to pursue those interests in language he had developed during his years at Dartmouth both in formal lessons and in the reading club of which he had been a member with James, Joseph Torrey, and John Wheeler, all of them now in Burlington and the latter two also with James at the university. Wheeler, in fact, succeeded James as president of the University of Vermont in 1833.

George's early interests in Scandinavian literature and languages

were renewed after the death of Harriet and young Charles in
1833. In October of that year he wrote to Carl Christian Rafn,
an eminent Danish philologist and antiquary, telling him of his
desire to acquire the "means of learning more of northern literary history."[15]

David Lowenthal has said that George Perkins Marsh's interest
in and fascination with the north had as many roots as the great
tree of Yggsdrasil.[16] These interests in things northern grew in
part out of his studies with James in German literature and philosophy both at Dartmouth and later in Burlington, where they
started up their reading club again from old undergraduate days.
They met, often at James's house, one or two nights in the week
to discuss Greek and German philosophy, the English Platonists
of the seventeenth century, and Coleridge—in 1830 James published an anthology entitled *Select Practical Theology of the
Seventeenth Century* and considered publishing selections from
Henry More, the Cambridge Platonist.[17] It was probably in these
years, as well as in earlier discussions with James at Dartmouth,
that George developed the organicist foundation of his thinking about the relations between man and the environment that
would come to fullest expression in his famous *Man and Nature*
(1864).

James's interests in foreign languages also continued during
the 1830s in Burlington. As a divinity student at Andover in
1821, his skill in German had led him to enter in his journal:
"Of my progress in the German language, I . . . begin to feel
as if I had conquered it."[18] In the summer of 1826 he completed his translation of Herder's *Spirit of Hebrew Poetry* for
serial publication in the *Biblical Repertory*, a journal published at
Princeton by members of the faculty there. Finally in 1833
he completed and saw published in Burlington a revised two-
volume edition of Herder, a book that the Brook Farmer George
Ripley in 1835 found valuable because it brought to New England an idea Herder had extended from Schleiermacher and
which Ripley found especially remedial to the stagnation of
religious thinking in the New England of the 1830s—"the soul's
sense of things divine."[19]

From swimming with James in what their friend Rufus Choate

in late 1818 had called "that ocean of German theology and
metaphysics,"[20] George's interests moved further north; and
soon after leaving Dartmouth he began buying books in Danish
and Icelandic and, until his eyes began to weaken, read widely
during 1820-21 in the Icelandic and other Scandinavian sagas.
After his initial interest in Scandinavia was renewed in 1833,
George's request for help from Rafn led in 1834 to the Dane in
turn enlisting Marsh as American secretary of the Danish Royal
Society of Northern Antiquaries. Marsh's role in the society was
to arouse interest and raise money for the publication of *Antiquitates Americanae*, a collection of sagas, codices, and other
materials relating to the Iceland-Greenland-Vinland voyages. In
good part through George's support of $500, as well as his pro-
motion of the project in America, *Antiquitates* was published
in 1837 and highly praised by Bostonians like Edward Everett
and T. W. Higginson.[21] Marsh was encouraged by the response
to this collection, so much so that he managed in 1838 to publish his *Compendious Grammar of the Old Northern or Icelandic
Language* (Burlington, 1838), a work based largely on his own
translation of Rasmus Christian Rask's Icelandic grammar, though
full of Marsh's own contributions.

Both Marshes' interests in languages comprehended the Coleridgean ideas that led James to publish *Aids to Reflection* in
1829 with his own "Preliminary Essay" explaining the value
of Coleridge's book to contemporary America. In that essay
James claimed that it was necessary to associate, as Coleridge
did but most Americans did not, "the study of words with the
study of morals and religion: and that is the most effectual method
of instruction, which enables the teacher most especially to fix
the attention upon a definite meaning . . . upon a particular act,
or process, or law of the mind—to call it into distinct conscious-
ness, and assign to it its proper name, so that the name shall
thenceforth have for the learner a distinct, definite and intelligible sense."[22]

The study of language as a means of moral instruction was
also at the base of George's growing interest in Icelandic and
Danish language and literature after the death of his wife and

son in 1833. He actually claimed a moral value for Scandinavian languages; and, as David Lowenthal shows, he ultimately affirmed the innate moral superiority of Germanic languages and peoples, including, with some real historiographic straining, their alleged Puritan descendants in early New England and even Marsh's purest Yankee nineteenth-century contemporaries. The Goth's, as he called early inhabitants of Scandinavia and northern Europe, "are the noblest branch of the Caucasian race. We are their children. . . . the spirit of the Goth," he claimed in 1843, "guided the May Flower across the trackless ocean."[23]

James and George, sons of aspirant aristocratic "founding fathers" of Vermont, revealed their nativist moral snobbery toward other than Anglo-Saxon-descended New Englanders more than once during the late thirties and early forties. In *The Goths in New England* (1843), George claimed high levels of morality for the Goths and, so he claimed by extension, their New England descendants. James, for his part, in his characterization of the Canadian French to brother-in-law David Read in 1837, similarly subscribed to a set of social attitudes that were American nativist, anti-Catholic, and based partly in German idealism and Herderean ethnocentric historicism. With little direct experience of the people, James told Read that the French of Lower Canada "certainly have no strength of religious or even moral principle," and "nine tenths of them can neither read nor write." Unlike New England's descendants of the Goths, "the Canadians as a people are utterly incapable of self-government."[24] Acclaiming the virtues of an Anglo-Saxon rural life of letters and reflection and democratic self-government based on Nordic models, the Marshes, as Hampdens of the Champlain Valley and self-imputed heirs of Snorri Sturluson, were pleased when their own political views were confirmed by public action, as when the General Assembly agreed to James's proposal that the university's direction, through its board of corporators, be removed from popular control in 1829 by an act of the legislature making the Board self-perpetuating and no longer responsible to a popularly elected assembly.

Yet while James's fears for the Congregational churches of

Vermont during the New Measure revivals of 1835 were in
good part an accurate prognosis of that institution's future
failure to determine Vermont's or New England's direction
as a community, the limitations both men suffered from as
direct heirs of an elite with aspirations to rule in an age when
the very notion of a ruling class could never be politically
acceptable caused them to misunderstand, for example, the
important and valuable larger functions of revivals in a young,
growing United States, or the formative contribution of the
Patriote War to the shaping of modern Canada.

In interests and thinking, then, the Marsh cousins were
closely sympathetic. Their responses to both Burchard and
Vermont's philo*patriotes* were of a piece. As David Lowenthal remarked of both men, James and George Perkins Marsh
"loathed sham and self deceit and held out no hope for the
perfectibility of man."[25] With James's death from tuberculosis
in 1842 and George's successful campaign for election to Congress later that year which would take him to Washington for
three terms until 1849, a passage in the story of Vermont's and
especially Burlington's cultural and intellectual life came to an
end. During a decade marked by intense political and social
conflict, fear of riot, war and violence, as well as deeply moving
personal disasters for both men, James and George Perkins
Marsh's intellectual interests and scholarship and their critical
responses to important social and political phenomena in Vermont, such as the New Measure revivals and the responses to
the *Patriote* War, demonstrate what John Dewey clearly recognized in James in his comments on the one hundredth anniversary of the publication in Burlington of Coleridge's *Aids to
Reflection:* "a wistful aspiration for full and ordered living."[26]

Alonzo Jackman (1809-79) of Norwich University, though
for most of his life an academic like the Marshes, presents an
interesting contrast with these slightly older men. Jackman
had none of the Marshes' social advantages in his childhood and,
in fact, after the death of his father and his mother's remar-
riage, was told at the age of twelve to "go and shift for himself."[27] He worked on a farm in Thetford, Vermont, for six

years and then went in 1827 with his brother to Chatham,
Connecticut, to work in a quarry. Unlike James Marsh, Jackman
was strong and healthy and thus able to make a living first in
the quarry and then on the Ohio River as a steamboat deck-
hand. Next he worked as a sailor on a coastal freighter in the
Gulf of Mexico and finally, heading back to Vermont, stopped
in New York to work for some months as a sailor on another
coastal freighter. He returned to Vermont in 1833 in search of
an education, one he quickly acquired at Alden Partridge's
Norwich University, graduating from the military college in
1836 to be hired by Partridge at the age of twenty-eight as
an instructor in mathematics.

Except for two periods totalling six years, the first when he
left the college in 1841 to start a short-lived school in Windsor, and then in 1849 to chase west after gold, Jackman taught
mathematics and science, civil engineering, and military science
at Norwich until his death in 1879. Colonel Partridge's scheme
for educating American democrats in the 1830s called for a
heavy dose of military training in the curriculum, an experience
which included lengthy marches, or "excursions" as Partridge
preferred to call them, during the college's summer vacations.
These body-building and mentally disciplining field trips, often
including some lectures on botany, geology, and military science
by accompanying faculty, led the troops across Vermont into
New York or east into New Hampshire. They were exercises,
Partridge believed, intended to form a trained citizenry able
to assume leadership and other active roles their young society
would demand of educated Americans. Jackman went on these
"excursions" both as cadet and faculty member. But, in late
August 1838 he took one trip of special interest on which he
was, as he said at the beginning of the journal he kept of his
trip to Quebec, "independent of company and alone."[28] It
was a foot, steamboat, rail, and stagecoach journey that took
him across Vermont's Green Mountains and over Lake Champlain to Fort Ticonderoga and Fort St. Frederic at Crown Point
in New York. From there he headed north by steamboat to
Saint John on the Richelieu River in Canada; then by train to
La Prairie on the Saint Lawrence River's south shore opposite

Montreal. After visiting Montreal, the journey down river to
Quebec brought him to the scene of another North American battlefield on the Plains of Abraham; and from there he
returned to Montreal and south to Burlington, walking then
to Norwich by way of the state capital at Montpelier. It was
a rapid, almost double-time march of nearly eight hundred miles
to Quebec and back in twelve days on which he accomplished
fully recorded observations of the countryside and military
fortifications at both former and present outposts of an England
which many Americans feared might soon be their wartime
enemy once again.

The great excitement on the Vermont-Canadian border during
the winter of 1837-38 had turned calm by late summer. Most
of the armed encounters between *patriotes* and British regulars
and loyal Canadian militia in Lower Canada had occurred earlier
in the winter. Robert Nelson's "great wolf hunt" would not
push north into the Richelieu River Valley until November.
Travelling as far as Montreal in his Norwich University faculty
uniform and later in mufti, Jackman seems to have passed
through the Canadian cities and countryside with few obstruc-
tions, though he does mention that "soon after entering Mon-
treall I saw it necessary to change my uniform for a citizens
dress, after which I was taken for an Englishman, hence passed
off very well."[29] His uniform, apparently suggesting an American army officer, could have engendered hostility from loyal
British Canadians.

Earlier, on the leg of his trip to Ticonderoga, Jackman stopped
in Shoreham to visit Governor Silas Jenison and there received
a letter of introduction to Lord Durham in Quebec. Jackman's
journal of his trip does not mention a visit to Durham, but he
easily managed to obtain a pass from the British military to
visit Cape Diamond, "the citidell" of Quebec, and, as he noted
in his journal, "saw the strength and review of the soldiers."[30]
In Montreal he also visited "the English troops and went into
their barrax and saw their order—soldiers appeared like good
hearted fellows. One showed me two peaces [*sic*, of cannon]
which were taken from the patriots last winter" (p. 253). The
cannon could have been those which Governor Jenison accused

Alec Catlin of knowing how to recover after they had been
given to the *patriotes* by the Stowe militia company. Jenison
wanted them returned because he feared a war with England.

A Yankee traveller who clearly knew he was visiting a foreign
land, Jackman commented on British political arrangements in
Canada. Saint Helen's Island in the Saint Lawrence River, he
remarked, contained "a fort to keep the city [of Montreal] in
check . . . which gives evidence that the English government is
not made for the people, but the people are made for the government. Is all this right to a free thinking American?" (p. 253.) Although he was not on his first trip out of Vermont, Jackman
nonetheless displayed native provincialism when, after remark-
ing that "never before [had he seen] a section of country, apparently so pleasant as the region from Montreal to Quebeck,"
he claimed to be "astonished to see in market all kinds, apparently, of vegetables that are in the states, as mellons, cucum-
bers etc. etc." (p. 257). His Protestant bias also came to the
surface in a stock response to the cathedral of French Catholic
Montreal, an architecturally interesting place for him, yet a
place where "people are constantly going in . . . for, in my
opinion, superstitious worship" (p. 253). His own church attendance on Sunday, September 2nd, was curtailed because
he had to see an important landmark. With a New Yorker
named Curtis he attended only morning services in the Methodist
Episcopal Church at Quebec for "though conscience stricken
[he] went to see [the falls of Montmorency] in company with
Mr. Curtis" during the afternoon (p. 255).

It is clear that Jackman was an observant traveller with a
special purpose for his trip. His responses to the landscapes of
his native Vermont and then to Canada are markedly contrastive.
In Vermont his comments are cliches; in Quebec they are detailed, precise, and purposeful. For example, he records a detailed and imaginative plan for attacking the Citadel at Cape
Diamond; and he earlier had noted Ticonderoga's vulnerability
to damaging fire from the higher ground of Mount Defiance to
the southwest. Early on his journey, however, as he headed
west across the central mountain range of Vermont, Jackman
duly recorded his comments on the mountain scenery in the

cliches of romantic landscape views. "The White River," Jackman notes, "ran with serpentine winding among a huge pile of
hills upon each side thrown together, and high peaks looking
over each other with terific [sic] wildness, all combined, formed
a grand romantic scenery." (p. 248). In Canada he similarly remarks on the falls of Montmorency when he "saw the broad-
ist [sic] and most beautiful rainbow I ever saw or imagined.
This was truly a romantic scenery" (p. 255). But the first
Canadian mountain he sighted between Chambly and Longeuil
is noted for having served as the scene of a *patriote* victory
during the previous winter. Moreover, his speculations on attacking the Citadel of Quebec are lively and sufficiently precise in conception to create a picture of himself as indeed
Partridge's travelling democratic citizen-soldier.

Yet the planning and military tactics, as well as the warrior's
rhetoric, provide some curious contrasts with his actual experience as an officer under arms. While in Quebec Jackman
noted that the inferior bravery of the defenders of the Citadel, which his plan of attack by balloons would subdue, came
about because the British and Canadians are "habituated to
be governed by a monarchical form. . . . If they were democrats, you might as well drive a tiger from his den as to move
the citizens . . ." (p. 256). Yet citizen-soldier Jackman never
himself raised a gun against an enemy in his entire military
career. During the two occasions when active military duty
called, he did not leave New England. Jackman went under
arms no further from Norwich than the Vermont-Canadian
border late in 1838 to command a militia unit sent by Governor Jenison to cooperate with federal troops under General
Wool in the enforcement of American neutrality. In 1847 he
took command of the New Hampshire militia during the Mexi-
can War; but after his seafaring days he never left the northeast
again until 1849 when he went to California in search of gold.

The connection between the Canadian *patriotes* and the men
of Alden Partridge's military college can only be reconstructed
in dim outline; but it appears to have been complicated; marked

with the suggestions of promised adventure which would attract young men both to the college and then to military escapades along the border to the north. Jackman, for example, certainly sounded and acted like a spy gathering important military information prior to a war with England and an invasion of Canada. The record does not reveal whether he was sent on an official mission or was compelled by his own personal sense of adventure and a need to risk danger. Yet his fellow alumni and students seem also to have been similarly drawn into the Canadian affair.

Cyrus Myrick (1817-1904) of Bridport, Vermont, was one such young man attracted to adventure. In the early stages of Jackman's journey to Quebec in 1838, he and Myrick met at Bridport, a few miles south of Middlebury, and went together to Governor Jenison's home in Shoreham, where Jackman received the letter of introduction to Lord Durham, and then across the lake together to view the ruins of Fort Ticonderoga and Fort St. Frederic, going on from there to visit another Norwich man, Jonathan Tarbell (1820-88), Class of 1839, in Moriah, New York. Soon after Jackman left by steamboat for Saint John, Myrick joined the *patriotes* near the border in Vermont where he put to use the few military skills he had acquired in the one year he attended Norwich. The *patriotes* took him on as drill master in preparation for the "great wolf hunt" later in 1838. Whether he drilled the troops in French, English, or both is not known. In fact, the historians of Norwich tell us only that Myrick was engaged in military action and "had many narrow escapes," but never what, when, or where Myrick escaped.[32]

A number of other Norwich graduates served in the regular army during the years 1837-38 on assignments along the Canadian border as part of President Van Buren's measures to enforce his neutrality proclamation. Peter Hagner (1815-93), Class of 1832, was second lieutenant in July 1838 on duty at the border in Wisconsin and later in Sacketts Harbor, New York. Samuel Ridgely (1809-59), Class of 1827, was also on the border patrolling during the Canadian Rebellions. But while these men were either regular army officers assigned to patrol the frontier or, like

Myrick, openly allied with the *patriotes* on border incursions back into Canada, Orin Marsh (1802-71), Class of 1825, showed the most original combination of allegiances. Living in Battle Creek, Michigan in 1838, Marsh, who was no relation to James or George Perkins Marsh, was commissioned Captain, Company A, 1st Regiment, Michigan Militia. But then, on October 29, 1839, he was commissioned Captain of Riflemen, First Regiment, First Brigade, First Division of the Patriots Army of Upper Canada, though continuing to hold his commission in the Michigan militia. His love of liberty and adventure, apparently, could thus pull him back and forth across the border to whichever military force required his services.

The living example of the liberty-loving, adventure-seeking Vermonter to whom Partridge's young citizen-soldiers could turn for a model in 1837-38 was a successful lawyer in Montpelier and trustee of the military college, Colonel Jonathan Peckham Miller (1797-1847). Miller saw his first military service in Captain Lebbeus Egerton's militia company of Randolph, Vermont, in the War of 1812 at the Battle of Plattsburgh during September 1814. After five years of service as a private in the regular army, however, Miller came back to Vermont, like Jackman a few years later, in search of an education. He stuttered through his first attempts, attending the Nutting brothers' academy in Randolph, then Dartmouth College for only a few weeks, and finally in 1821 enrolling in the University of Vermont where he stayed until the main college building burned down in the spring of 1824.

Hearing of the Greek revolt against Turkey, Miller joined the Greek Committee of Boston and was sent to join Lord Byron and the revolutionaries at Missolonghi in late 1824.[33] Byron died before Miller's arrival, but the Vermonter commanded a brigade of what had been Byron's troops and at the siege of Missolonghi in 1826 earned the title, "American Daredevil," for his feats of bravery.[34] In late 1826 Miller toured the United States to solicit help for the Greeks, and then returned to Greece in 1827 to take charge of distributing relief supplies sent from America. During these adventures, Miller came to possess the sword Byron had carried during the Greek campaign.

By 1830, Miller had returned to America, read for and been admitted to the bar, established a law practice in Montpelier, and in 1832 was elected to the Vermont General Assembly. Bringing his fervor for freedom home to Vermont, he introduced a resolution to the General Assembly calling on Vermont's congressional delegation to work toward the abolition of slavery in the District of Columbia in 1833. Strongly antislavery, Miller was a delegate to London's World Anti-Slavery Convention in 1840.

If Jonathan Peckham Miller had an active role on the Vermont side of supporting the Canadian *patriotes*, it is difficult to say today. But that he was a figure Partridge and his faculty could point to and urge their students to emulate would seem likely. Students could not fail to see in Miller a man of action, a lover of freedom and liberty whom their college honored by entrusting him with its interests. Moreover, the students of Norwich and other Vermonters could find in Jonathan Miller a living model of the American citizen who had indeed fought for freedom in their own lifetime.

Miller's Montpelier neighbor and fellow lawyer, Daniel Pierce Thompson, left in his novel, *The Green Mountain Boys* (1839), a fully developed literary image of Vermonters as freedom-loving men of action.[35] Just as William Gilmore Simms in South Carolina and James Fenimore Cooper in New York turned to the heroic revolutionary or colonial past of their regions, Thompson fully exploited associationist aesthetics in his own historical novel, using a loose reading of the facts and characters from Vermont's revolutionary past, Ethan and Ira Allen, and the military force they led through the region during the Revolution to engage the British at the capture of Fort Ticonderoga and the battles of Hubbardton and Bennington. Thompson, moreover, with Miller, Hiland Hall of Bennington, and Henry Stevens, Sr., had been prominent among the founders of the Vermont Historical Society. With Vermont's English-language past less than eighty years old, the Vermont Historical Society's avowed purpose of "preserving and disseminating" the story of Vermont's past was a self-conscious effort to establish a deposited account of a particular people, events, and, with the society's commitment to

publishing early records, discourses with all the attendant and
necessary rhetoric against which the present could measure itself and seek inspiration when it faced troublesome times.

Thompson's *Green Mountain Boys* was quickly accepted by
readers, and its characters and events became staples of Vermont's popular historical fiction for the remainder of the nineteenth century, for Thompson's audience had been ready for
him. Alonzo Jackman, for example, when he visited Ticonderoga,
suggested that the soil for Thompson had already been tilled
and fertilized by "the hero of Ti' " himself, Ethan Allen, when
Jackman, upon viewing the "old fort, now nearly demolished
by the hand of time," noted the place "where Col. Allen entered
and where he caused the garison [*sic*] to surrender by his thunder-
ing voice" ("Journal," p. 250). Allen, in his own account of that
event, reminded his readers, first, that his motivations were of
the highest order: "Ever since I arrived to a state of manhood,
and acquainted myself with the general history of mankind,
I have felt a sincere passion for liberty." Then, in his account
of the fort's surrender, Allen dramatically posed himself before
the door of British Captain Delaplace's quarters and ordered him
"to come forth instantly, or I would sacrifice the whole garrison."
Delaplace, breeches in hand, as Allen recreated the scene, questioned the Yankee's authority, to which Allen replied with an
all-embracing authority appropriate to his increasingly heroic
stature as he stood before the pantless British officer: "In the
name of the great Jehovah, and the Continental Congress." When
Delaplace still resisted, Allen drew his sword and "demanded
an immediate surrender of the garrison." Delaplace promptly
complied. Thus, as Jackman then and many Vermonters still
recall, Allen achieved the surrender of the fort "by the thunder-
ing of his voice."[36]

But, even as a fictional self-promotion, Allen's version of the
capture of Ticonderoga had an appealingly truthful ring to it.
It *had* to happen that way, even if it did not. Thompson's later
version of Allen and the Green Mountain Boys had to work
hard to live up to Allen's own creation of himself; and, as a
result, Ethan Allen in the 1830s rumbles rather than thunders.

As the Green Mountain Boys "merrily sped their way to the western shore" of Lake Dunmore in the novel's opening scene, one of them characterized Colonel Allen: "Lordy! why, two Alexanders, with half a dozen Turks thrown in to stiffen the upper lip, would be used up in making the priming to Ethan Allen." Later, in preparation for defeating a squad of New York militiamen in a drinking bout, Allen is brought on the scene in blatantly heroic figures, though no likeness of him exists.

Of an uncommon height, and with an extraordinary breadth of chest, supplied with large brawny limbs, his whole frame constituted a figure of the most Herculean cast; while his large, darkly bright eyes, and the air of intelligence that marked the general expression of his coarse, lion-like features, gave evidence that his intellectual powers were not, as frequently occurs in such instances, wholly incommensurate with his physical proportions. A modern phrenologist, indeed, while comparing his high and remarkably expansive forehead, with the vast volume which composed the back part of his head, might be much puzzled to decide whether his intellectual or animal nature would most predominate in his character. His dress, which was likewise somewhat singular for the times, consisted of high, heavy boots, buff breeches and doublet, with a high-collared, white shag coat of the frock kind, all of which was surmounted by a fine, though much worn beaver, slouched, except for the front part, which was turned up so as to give an additional boldness to his large features, and to impart somewhat of a bandit aspect to his appearance. This, to observation, completed his outward equipment; though a closer inspection might have revealed the shape of a stout pistol swelling the smooth and snugly setting leather over each of his breeches pockets, while the buck-horn handle of a large war-knife might occasionally be seen protruding from its sheath attached to the side lining of his coat.

Placing the heavy rifle which he bore in his hand in a corner, the stranger now advanced, and, with an air of easy

unconcern, seated himself by the side of his host in the
family circle round the fire.[37]

A hero, then, of brains, brawn, controlled violence, and easy
democratic manner, Ethan Allen in the 1830s is of requisite
size and character.

But as the 1840s come on and trouble seems to recede into
the past, however temporarily and even if only to be replaced
by new disturbances as the nation and Vermont move toward
a resolution of the question of slavery which looms with increasing threat over the nation, Vermonters turned to a leader
of decidedly un-Ethan Allenish dimensions, behavior, or quality.
Silas Jenison (1791-1849) of Shoreham had become acting governor in 1835 through the decisive persuasion of George Perkins
Marsh in the Vermont General Assembly when the assembly
failed in thirty-six ballots to elect William Palmer, winner of
only a plurality in the popular election, governor of Vermont.
Jenison won the governorship in his own right in 1836 and then,
in 1838, in his second elected term, earned the wrath of the
philo*patriotes* for granting the anti*patriote* petition of George
Perkins Marsh and others, and subsequently declaring Vermont's
neutrality with the assurances of whatever militia he could muster into dependable service with the federal force of General
John Ellis Wool. But Jenison had also acquired a reputation for
measured phrase and action. He grew up on a farm managed by
his mother, who was widowed when he was only one year old.
Though only a common school student in his childhood, Jenison
later learned Latin, French, algebra, and surveying (a skill he
turned to employment before and after his political career) from
Gideon Sessions, a retired schoolmaster living in Shoreham.
Despite the enmity of philo*patriotès* for calling out the militia
against them in 1838, Vermonters thought well enough of steady
Silas Jenison to reelect him for a third term with the largest
majority vote for any governor of Vermont elected to that date.
He, too, served as trustee of Norwich University during these
years.[38]

There may be only a tenuous relationship between the ver-
balizing of ideas, such as invoking the spirit of the Green Moun-

tain Boys or professing a newly awakened faith in Jesus, and
launching an armed attack against British regulars in support of
liberty-seeking *patriotes* or giving up rum and deer hunting on
Sunday in order to go to church meeting and otherwise lead
a good Christian life. The contrast in the 1830s between ideational rhetoric and reality was probably no greater than at any
other time in the nineteenth century until the Civil War. Yet
the growing weight of the rhetoric, when it became institutionalized through agencies like the Vermont Historical Society and
broadcast in newspaper reports of philo*patriotes'* resolutions or
later in fiction like Thompson's *Green Mountain Boys,* resulted
in the growing conviction that rhetoric was reality. Likewise,
in the New Measure and other revivals of the Second Great
Awakening, new converts, just as Jedidiah Burchard said, were
not drawn to Christ through ideas, although the rhetoric of the
ideal Christian experience, union with Christ and his saints in a
holy community, can be found in any revival sermon or hymn.
The rhetoric of the past, often presented by writers like Daniel
Pierce Thompson, convinced listeners in the present that the
rhetoric was the sole cause of the early act, and thus more easily
impelled their later action.

Indeed, the force of real considerations as against ideal considerations in making public and private decisions correlates
with the degree of abstraction of the action to be decided. As
one of Vermont's philo*patriotes* remarked, he was *for* the rebels,
but when it came to real action, he wanted a leader like George
Washington, now dead at least forty years and thus a safe name
to invoke in rhetorical justification of both his ideal revolutionary spirit and his real absence from the battle scene.

NOTES

1. David Lowenthal, *George Perkins Marsh: Versatile Vermonter*
(New York, 1958), 2-7.

2. *The Remains of the Rev. James Marsh* . . . , ed. by Joseph Torrey
(Boston, 1843), 13.

3. On these and earlier years at Dartmouth, *see* Fred Chase, *A History
of Dartmouth College* (Cambridge, Mass., 1891); *CAD*, 9-12.

4. Torrey, *Remains,* 15-17.

5. Ibid., 44-47.
6. Ibid., 28.
7. *CAD*, 12.
8. Ibid., 44.
9. Ibid., 58-68.
10. Lowenthal, *George Perkins Marsh*, 5.
11. Ibid., 4.
12. Ibid., 43-45.
13. *CAD*, 172.
14. Torrey, *Remains*, 110-15.
15. Lowenthal, *George Perkins Marsh*, 43.
16. Ibid., 44.
17. *CAD*, 21-24.
18. Torrey, *Remains*, 37.
19. George Ripley in *The Christian Examiner*, 38 (May 1835), 170.
20. Torrey, *Remains*, 69.
21. Lowenthal, *George Perkins Marsh*, 46.
22. Samuel Taylor Coleridge, *Aids to Reflection, in the formation of a Manly Character, on the Several Grounds of Prudence, Morality, and Religion; illustrated by select passages from our elder divines, especially from Archbishop Leighton*. 1st American ed. (Burlington, Vt., 1829), viii.
23. Lowenthal, *George Perkins Marsh*, 9.
24. *CAD*, 195.
25. Lowenthal, *George Perkins Marsh*, 39.
26. John Dewey's address at UVM in 1929 on the one hundredth anniversary of Marsh's edition of *Aids to Reflection* was published twice later, in the *Journal of the History of Ideas*, 2 (1941), and *Problems of Men* (New York, 1946).
27. *Norwich University/1819-1911/Her History, Her Graduates, Her Roll of Honor*, ed. by William Arba Ellis, Vol. 2, 1820-66 (Montpelier, Vt., 1911), 267-70.
28. "Journal of Alonzo Jackman's Excursion to Quebec, 1838," ed. by Gary T. Lord, *Vermont History*, 46 (Fall 1978), 246.
29. Ibid., 253.
30. Ibid., 255.
31. Ellis, *Norwich University*, 269.
32. Ibid., 321.
33. Ibid., 9-10.
34. Ibid., 10.
35. Daniel Pierce Thompson, *The Green Mountain Boys* (Montpelier, Vt., 1839).
36. Ethan Allen, "The Capture of Fort Ticonderoga," from *A Narrative of Col. Ethan Allen's Captivity* (Walpole, N.H., 1807), 13-21.
37. Thompson, *Green Mountain Boys*, 125.
38. Ellis, *Norwich University*, 7.

CHAPTER SEVEN

PHAEDON OR BOWDITCH

People suffering from ambiguous or confusing social strains subscribe easily to the panaceas offered in evangelism, whether political or religious. The makeup of a strained social situation could include both people with no religious or political orientation who desperately need one, and people with orientations, political, social, or religious, so rigid that social pressures, in the form of propagandizing or preaching, serve only to strengthen them.[1] A dominant characteristic of the half century following the American Revolution was the rise of an expressive self-consciousness generated in part by the ambiguities of change. Patriotic experiments in literature and fine arts, for example, reflect what Benjamin Spencer called a self-conscious "quest for nationality" and what psychologists could point to as verbal and visual symptoms of a people undergoing crisis.[2] The literature of the "quest for nationality" illustrates all of the characteristics of ideological preaching; and one of the most important sermons was Emerson's *The American Scholar*. The salient arguments of Emerson's address to Harvard's Phi Beta Kappa chapter in 1838 formed, in Spencer's words, "a synthesis of what had been developed by scores of authors in the two preceding decades."[3] Since at least the War of 1812 Americans had been the actors and the audience in extended attempts to formulate an ideological frame of reference for their own national identity. These efforts can bear brief repeating, for in these attempts to establish an intellectual and aesthetic frame of reference for a national identity can be found ideological correlatives for the social responses to events such as the *Patriote* War and Burchard's revivals.

The relationship of ideology to group identity lies in those elements that can link individuals into a common identity or nationality. When an ideology is compelling in its power, promises a revival of some traditional force, permits even the cynical to appear sincere, has the sanction of righteousness, promises individuals a role in the reconstruction of society, and gives a total meaning to the individual's image of the world, the aggressive and discriminative energies of the individual become harnessed into a group identity.[4] In whatever lasting or transitory form it takes, ideology is a necessity for the growing ego; moreover, it promises, in a simplification of historical perspective, "salvation, conquest, reform, happiness, rationality, and technological mastery," or in the rhetoric of the *patriotes* and their Vermont supporters, a struggle of "Principle . . . a struggle for the overthrow of a monarchical, and the establishment of a republican form of government."[5]

The intensity of the demand for an American commitment to ideology in 1837 impelled Charles Ingersoll, in an address to the American Philosophical Society entitled "A Discourse Concerning the Influence of America on the Mind," to cry, "Give us, then, *nationality* . . . ; Give us excess of it."[6] The literature of the years after the War of 1812 resounds with variants of that *cri de coeur*. By calling for an American self-assertiveness, a writer like James Fenimore Cooper expressed his need for a national ideology which could give him a world of shared experience and a frame of reference with other Americans. Cooper, often America's most anglophobic writer, found the English influence on American culture paralyzing. He felt himself compelled to lay "the foundation of the mental emancipation which alone can render the nation great by raising its opinion to the level of its facts."[7]

The adolescent stage of America's development was acknowledged time and again. America, a "new country, with a new history," William Cullen Bryant said, should have literary expressions of her youth arise from her actual conditions. He characterized American poetry as a "newborn being," at times awkward and affected (as his own efforts attested) but still "full of youth and life."[8] John Neal ambivalently called for American literature to show itself: "come forth naked, absolutely naked . . . though your muscles be too large. . . ." Then, correcting himself in order to comply with current proprieties and sexual decorums, Neal called for the Belvidere Apollo to appear in Yankee clothes, "breeches; or, if that be much too 'coarse,' in 'shorts,' or 'tights,' or 'inexpressibles.'"[9]

Cooper tried hard to find American building material for the "foundation of mental emancipation" he sought to erect by returning to the Revolution in *The Spy* and using Indian and frontier material in the "Leatherstocking Tales." But he did not entirely achieve his own emancipation. For all of Cooper's use of Revolutionary War and colonial themes, Walter Scott and the association psychology of Scott's countrymen gave direction to Cooper and many other American writers in the early nineteenth century.[10] Orestes Brownson had insisted that "God had selected the American people to point the way to universal freedom and American writers to embody this idea in their works," and the Yale poet, James Hillhouse, saw American authors as the "left arm of a nation whose mission it was to become the 'Viceregent of Eternal Justice' among all men."[11] But, in fact, the ideological framework which would inform such a gesture continued in the years after the War of 1812 to rely on Europe despite Cooper's efforts to emancipate the American mind.

Even though many American intellectuals repeatedly accused England of exercising a dominant cultural influence on the United States, the erstwhile mother country shared that role.

Germany and Scotland also exerted important influences, but
in contradictory ways. While they both contributed ideas to
building an American ideology, they also simultaneously contributed to a confusion and conflict in its terms. When, beginning in 1815, men like George Bancroft, Edward Everett, and
George Ticknor joined the stream of Americans travelling to
Europe in order to study at German universities, young America encountered ideas about literature and history which would
soon seem perfectly suited to their attempts to formulate an
ideology congenial with the emerging expressions of American
society fast establishing themselves under the rubric of Jacksonian Democracy, expressions at once embodying European
reform and indigenous American development and easily adapted
north of the Canadian-United States boundary. The fiery William
Lyon Mackenzie, leader of the Upper Canadian rebels, had made
a pilgrimage to Washington to see Andrew Jackson. Papineau and
his *patriote* followers also closely followed the American scene
and like Mackenzie responded to the appeal of Jacksonian ideology. The rhetoric of Jacksonian Democracy easily found its way
into their political baggage.[12]

George Ticknor enthusiastically reported on the freedom of
ideas in German universities where he heard the voice of popular
feeling express itself. The literary doctrines he learned at Götting-
en, particularly from Dissen, Schultze, and other disciples of
Herder, provided him the necessary justifications for the popular
voice.[13] If, as Herder said, the poetry of the Bible spoke from the
spirit of the Hebrew people, so too the mass of popular literature
being published in the land of that other chosen people, democratic America, spoke from the popular spirit. A Boston Brahmin
like Ticknor might have been uneasy with the country humor of
"The Big Bear of Arkansas" and other almanac fiction published
in the 1830s or the down east twang of Jack Downing's con-
versations with "the Giniral"; but ideas about reforming education gleaned from his German experience could give even those
crude artifacts of a democratic culture a place in the development of an American national ideology.[14] So, not many years
after returning from Europe and while advising Jefferson on

teaching languages at the old sage's newly established University
of Virginia, Ticknor attempted in the mid-1820s at Harvard his
own democratic reforms based on German ideas. Freedom of
choice in electing courses, advancement at the student's own
rate of progress, and the general abolition of externally imposed
classifications in favor of promoting the organic growth of
knowledge, Ticknor believed, would allow the mind and spirit
to develop fully.[15] Never more than partial, Ticknor's reforms
of Harvard's curriculum were confined to his own department
of romance languages where his students' examinations demonstrated an improvement in learning languages. Harvard resisted
his German theories of educational reform and would not allow
a general elective system until 1841, six years after Ticknor had
left the college for the private life of an independent man of
letters.[16] Even this liberalization of the curriculum proved short-
lived; Jared Sparks restored a restrictive curriculum when he
assumed the presidency in 1846.[17]

At the University of Vermont a similar educational debate occupied Professor James Marsh, who gradually revised the curriculum according to a model he found in an essay by Samuel
Taylor Coleridge. He corresponded on educational theory with
his friend Ticknor for nearly a decade with the same intensity
exhibited in the shorter series of letters to his brother-in-law,
David Read, concerning the *Patriote* War. Marsh's democratic
curricular reforms went beyond Ticknor's and even included a
pioneering version of continuing education, by offering courses
designed for the citizens of Burlington. Unhappily, as at Harvard,
reform collapsed. The populace did not support Marsh's vision
of well-educated, divinely inspired democrats; instead they
wanted unvarnished, practical carpenters, masons, or merchants.[18]

By the mid-1830s the acceptance of German philosophical
and literary doctrines, however, went far beyond a coterie of
American doctors of philosophy educated at Göttingen. As
Frederick Henry Hedge recalled of the first meeting of the group
that eventually called itself the Transcendental Club, the air of
Boston was alive with German thought in 1836.[19] The spell that
Immanuel Kant cast on the minds of some Americans in the

1830s had been emphasized by Hedge in 1833 when he tried to
define "the key to the whole critical philosophy of Kant and
the German School, the very essence of which consists in proposing an absolute self as unconditionally existing [and] incapable of being determined by anything higher than itself but
determining all things through itself." For Hedge and his Boston
friends, the major contributions of German philosophy were
"the moral liberty proclaimed by Kant as it had never been
proclaimed by any before; the authority and evidence of law
and duty set forth by Fichte; the universal harmony illustrated
by Schelling."[20]

While many of the ideas from Germany that Emerson, the
future Brook Farmer George Ripley, Hedge, and others found
attractive were also transmitted through English channels, prin-
cipally in the writings of Samuel Taylor Coleridge and Thomas
Carlyle, even Americans who had not been to Europe, like
James Marsh, made their own contributions. When Marsh's
translation of Herder's *Spirit of Hebrew Poetry* appeared in
two volumes in 1833, seven years after its apparently unnoticed
serial publication in the *Biblical Repertory*, George Ripley in
Boston acknowledged New England's debt to an American
scholar for introducing to these shores an idea Herder had extended from Schleiermacher into the study of Hebrew poetry—
"the soul's sense of things divine."[21] Not only would such a
doctrine contribute to the understanding of the special nature
of ancient Hebrew poetry, Ripley and others realized, it would
also give meaning to the developing concept of the importance
of the individual in a new nation where the uncertainty of the
time made that importance difficult to locate and define, though
often enough asserted.

Ideas from Herder, Kant, and other Germans, however, were
not everywhere so readily received nor considered important for
making sense out of American experience; and strongly expressed
resistance to the German influence emanated from such places as
Princeton, as well as Ripley's Boston. When Marsh first published
his translation of *Vom Geist der Ebraischen Poesie* in the *Biblical*

Repertory (1826), Charles Hodge, the magazine's editor, in a
note appended to the final installment, refused to accept the
German historian's point of view.[22] Hodge's resistance fore-
shadowed an anti-German campaign that would break out fully
in the late 1830s when Hodge, even though he had studied in
Germany from 1826 to 1828, and other Princeton men joined
with Andrews Norton, the strong-minded spokesman for Unitarian Orthodoxy, in the battle against Ripley and "the latest
form of infidelity" imported from Germany.[23]

The opposition to German philosophical imports, whether
they came in Marsh's translations, Coleridge's modifications,
or Carlyle's distortions, rested on a general acceptance of the
doctrines of the Scottish rhetoricians and Common Sense philosophers. While David Hume's *Treatise of Human Nature* (1739)
developed the theory of association, David Hartley achieved
the most thorough and influential application of it in *Observations of Man* (1745); for Hartley, ideas were generated by the
physical vibrations of the brain. He was concerned to show that
associations led men from a love of the world to "theopathy."
Seeking an ultimate source of those vibrations, however, led to
Hume's skepticism, an intolerable position for Orthodox Christians. Thus the Scottish philosopher Thomas Reid proposed a
theory of innate promptings of "Common Sense." Hugh Blair,
Lord Kames, and Archibald Alison mixed Hartleyian associa-
tional theory and Common Sense in stressing the role of the
perceiving mind at the expense of the thing perceived.

"The Scottish Enlightenment was probably the most potent
single tradition in the American Enlightenment," Herbert W.
Schneider has pointed out.[24] Writing from Vermont to Coleridge in 1829 as he prepared to republish the English poet-
philosopher's *Aids to Reflection* in Burlington, James Marsh
noted that "the Scotch writers . . . Steward [*sic*], Campbell
and Brown, are now almost universally read as the standard
authors on the subjects which they treat," philosophy and
psychology.[25] Moreover, the doctrines of the Scottish rhetoricians continued until after the Civil War to exert their more
formal influence across the land. Students from Dartmouth

College and the University of Vermont in northern New England to North Carolina and Transylvania in Kentucky were solidly grounded in Blair's *Rhetoric* and Kames's *Elements of Criticism*, and from at least the War of 1812 on they studied Alison's aesthetic theory based on the association of ideas.[26] The poet Richard Dabney paraphrased Alison in 1815 when he said that poetic association turns "a common occurrence of common scenery" into something beautiful. The "faculty of association, acting under the influence of Memory and Imagination" becomes the "messenger from soul to thought," and ennobles a barren scene.[27] Returning to the Revolution for the subject matter of their art or using Indian legends and frontier material, as Cooper or the South Carolinian William Gilmore Simms did, American artists were consistent with the theories of associationism, theories widely subscribed to by the 1830s. Objects and scenes from America's past and sometimes its present, especially its landscape, according to the aesthetics of associationism, would produce some simple emotion through an exercise of imagination or the faculty of association. Thus the individual could at once unite America's past and present, and experience that unity through the emotions evoked by an appropriately rendered scene or event.[28]

Both German and Scottish influences on American intellectual and cultural development by the 1830s, then, promised theoretical bases for American experience which would define the relationships of the individual and the physical and moral environment. Both were promising sources of ideas because they structured the individual act of perception and the thing perceived in a way that seemed to point to the ultimate unity of subject and object. But tendencies of German idealism and Scottish associationism pulled in different directions, and, at odds with each other, confused the quest for a group or national ideology. Subscribers to German Philosophical Idealism, as Melville's narrator warns when Ishmael stands watch in the crow's nest of the *Pequod*, could follow the worthless young sailor "with the Phaedon instead of Bowditch's" *Practical Navigator*:

Lulled into such an opium-like listlessness . . . this absent-
minded youth . . . at last loses his identity; takes the
mystic ocean at his feet for the visible image of that deep,
blue, bottomless soul, pervading mankind and nature, and
every strange, half-seen, gliding beautiful thing that eludes
him; every dimly discovered, uprising fin of some undis-
cernible form, seems to him the embodiment of those
elusive thoughts that only people the soul by continually
flitting through it. . . . But while this sleep, this dream is
on ye, move your foot or hand an inch; slip your hold at
all; and your identity comes back in horror. Over Descartian
vortices you hover. And perhaps, at mid-day, in the fairest
weather, with one half-throttled shriek you drop through
that transparent air into the summer sea, no more to rise
forever. Heed it well, ye Pantheists.[29]

Emerson had struck the transcendentalists' chord of pantheism
in 1834 when he concluded his poem "Each and All" with the
couplet:

Beauty through my senses stole;
I yielded myself to the perfect whole.[30]

Melville, on the other hand, clearly warned of a dangerous ten-
dency in philosophical idealism of totally diffusing an identity
when the individual became submerged in "the perfect whole."

Rhetoric based on the Scottish philosophers, however, tended
to encourage formal correctness and propriety, rather than sponta-
neity or suppleness in the use and criticism of language, thereby
frustrating the development of a native idiom for formulating
and expressing nationality.[31] Moreover, Alison's theory of associations was ambivalent in its implications. The Scottish rhetorician
proposed the emotion of beauty as the product of a succession of
agreeable ideas set up in the imagination by objects associated
with the simple emotions. Two kinds of association existed: universal associations, which had social and national implications;
and individual associations, which would allow the development

of theories about aesthetic subjectivity concerning both the artist
and his audience. Alison's ideas were applicable in a relatively
stable society, as in the American Era of Good Feelings that followed the War of 1812. But by the 1830s, Jacksonian America
obscured the linkage vital to a train of agreeable ideas, and with
bumptious, wildly divergent self-assertiveness, rendered Alison's
"universal" world meaningless and his ambivalent concept of
dubious value in constructing a national identity.

In England Alison's theory had made possible Wordsworth's
new concept of social values and provided a base for romantic
idealism. Wordsworth's readers in England had quickly come to
realize, especially with the help of the famous "Preface" to the
Lyrical Ballads, that the English poet's concept of nature not
only included an individual or private peculiarity, but also a
universal concept of religious and moral force in which nature
was both healer and teacher. In England, with its relatively
tamed countryside, such a concept of nature could have universal associations. The American landscape did not present
itself so uniformly as a source or object for universal associations, a familiar, predictable element, and instead could threaten
the very lives of those who would leave their cities to confront
it. American landscape, as yet untamed, in various stages of
cultivation and development, offered Americans an irregular
myriad of possibilities. Travelling through northern Vermont
in the spring of 1842, the youthful Francis Parkman attended
commencement at the University of Vermont and observed
the organized New England town of Burlington and its matur-
ing institutional life. A few miles to the east he walked under
a green canopy that enshrouded the stump-cluttered woods
of the Eastern Townships of Lower Canada and Orleans and
Essex Counties, Vermont. There as the guest of unlettered
and garrulous settlers he slept in one-room log cabins typical
of the first step in taming the still primeval northern New England forest. His experience in the north of Vermont previewed
the difficult and strength-consuming, dysentery-afflicted months
he would later spend on the Great Plains.[32]

America, therefore, tended to see Alison's systems and the

universals in Wordsworth's poetry it sanctioned mainly as arguments against private or subjective associations in poetry. A review of Wordsworth in the New York *Atlantic Magazine* said that Alison justified the function of criticism as a "study of the most prevalent and most permanent associations in the circle of art," but then castigated the critics of *Blackwood's Magazine* for praising the subjectivity of Coleridge's "Ancient Mariner." Associationism demanded from Americans an emphasis on universal experience perceived through proper forms in a time when, however, American democracy's conscious intentions to tolerate individual and plural moralities, for example, precluded homogeneity of universally accepted intellectual, social, or political values.[33]

By their counterthrusting tendencies, German and Scottish influences on American thought, despite a superficial similarity in which both seemed to offer a mode of synthesizing subject and object into an ultimately satisfying identity, thus intensified uncertainty and tension in the development of an American ideology and the quest for a national identity through the 1830s and on to the Civil War.

NOTES

1. Hadley Cantril, *The Psychology of Social Movements* (New York, 1941), 64-77.

2. Benjamin Spencer, *The Quest for Nationality* (Syracuse, 1957). The following discussion of American artists and writers is indebted to Spencer's important study of the "quest for nationality" aspects of antebellum American literature.

On the significance of cultural conditions and cultural products in the development of both personal and group or national identities, see H. Hartmann, E. Kris, and R. M. Lowenstein, "Some Psychoanalytic Comments on 'Culture and Personality,' " in G. B. Wilbur and W. Muensterberger, eds., *Psychoanalysis and Culture* (New York, 1951).

3. Spencer, *Quest for Nationality*, 150.

4. An individual manifests the turbulent and confused symptoms of identity crisis when, in Erikson's words, "Exposed to a combination of experiences which demands his simultaneous commitment to *physical intimacy* (not by any means always overtly sexual), to decisive *occupational choice*, to energetic *competition*, and to psychological definition."

Erik Erikson, "The Problem of Identity," in *Identity and Anxiety,* ed.
by M. P. Stern, A. J. Vidich, and D. M. White (Glencoe, Ill., 1960), 55,
80-81.

5. Ibid., 70; and *Burlington Sentinel,* February 22, 1838.

6. Ingersoll is quoted in Spencer, *Quest for Nationality,* 73. William
Ellery Channing's famous review-essay of Ingersoll's text of "The Influence of America on the Mind," published in the *Christian Examiner,*
36 (1830), 262-94, is an extension of Ingersoll's proposition that a nation's literature is the expression of national character. Channing's ideas
on the relationship of literature and aesthetics to national character are
examined in Daniel Howe's *The Unitarian Conscience; Harvard Moral
Philosophy 1805-1861* (Cambridge, Mass., 1970), 182-83. Channing
realized that the tension between nationalism and cosmopolitanism was
frustrating efforts to produce a national literature because Harvard Unitarians defined American national culture in European, mostly Scottish,
terms.

7. Quoted in Spencer, *Quest for Nationality,* 78.

8. Ibid., 129.

9. Spencer, *Quest for Nationality,* 129.

10. Ibid., 103.

11. Quoted in Spencer, *Quest for Nationality,* 125.

12. *See* G. M. Craig, "The American Impact on the Upper Canadian
Reform Movement before 1837," *Canadian Historical Review,* 29 (Dec-
ember, 1948); S. D. Clark, *Movements of Political Protest in Canada
1640-1840* (Toronto, 1959), chs. 15 and 16; Margaret Fairley, ed., *The
Selected Writings of William Lyon Mackenzie* (Toronto, 1960); and
Fernand Ouellet, "Papineau dans la Revolution de 1837-1838," *Canadian
Historical Association Annual Report,* 1958, 13-34. For a good example
of the Jacksonian tone in the *patriotes'* rhetoric, *see* Dr. Wolfred Nelson's
"Declaration of Independence," in the *Montreal Gazette,* March 6, 1838.

13. *Life, Letters, and Journals of George Ticknor* (Boston, 1880), I,
76-80, 99-120. From his discussions with Heeren, Dissen, and Schultze,
Ticknor came to believe that a nation's educational system should be an
organic part of its culture. He saw great faults in the German system, but
they seemed to stem mostly from the coarse personal and social behavior
of the German professors who affronted Ticknor's prudish Yankee sensi-
bility. Especially in the freedom and personal liberty of academic life in
Germany, however, Ticknor saw something that he believed needed trans-
porting to America.

14. On the implicit elitism of the aesthetics developed from Scottish
associationism by the Harvard moral philosophers, *see* Daniel Howe, *The
Unitarian Conscience,* 183-89.

15. Ticknor told James Marsh: "We divide and advance the sections
without any regard to the divisions of classes or distinctions between
graduates and undergraduates. We give full liberty of choice what they

will study and, indeed, whether they will study any modern language at all. And each section in each language is advanced according to its proficiencies, no person being permitted to leave off studying a language until he has learnt it and undergone a real examination. . . . At a late examination of about thirty in French, members of three classes were found in the same section, some of whom had been studying the language above two years, others a year and a half, and so on, till in one case an individual had studied it only three months. There was very little difference between them in attainment. . . . The system is successful and it is already producing its effect on others." *CAD*, 84-85; George Ticknor to James Marsh, April 14, 1829.

16. In February, 1841, Harvard adopted a system of elective courses in which at the end of the freshman year students could continue classical studies or pursue other courses in their place.

17. *Dictionary of American Biography*, XVII, 433.

18. The surviving correspondence between Marsh and Ticknor, deposited in the Baker Library, Dartmouth College and the Wilbur Collection, UVM, begins in 1822 when Marsh wrote an article for the *North-American Review* entitled "Ancient and Modern Poetry," apparently on Ticknor's invitation, and continues through Marsh's years on the faculty of Hampden-Sydney College and during his years of reforming UVM's curriculum in the late 1820s and early 1830s.

See also Julian Ira Lindsay, *Tradition Looks Forward/The University of Vermont/A History 1791-1904* (Burlington, Vt., 1954), ch. 12, for a discussion of the German-Coleridgean design of UVM's curriculum in the 1830s.

19. "The writings of Coleridge, recently edited by Marsh," Hedge recalled, "and some of Carlyle's earlier essays. . . . had created a ferment in the minds of the younger clergy of the day. There was a promise in the air of a new era of intellectual life." Quoted in James Eliot Cabot, *A Memoir of Ralph Waldo Emerson* (Boston, 1887), 244-45.

20. F. H. Hedge, "Coleridge's Literary Character," *Christian Examiner*, 14 (1833), 108-29. The first ten pages of this review-essay, occasioned by the American edition of Coleridge's *Biographia Literaria* (1817) and James Marsh's edition of *Aids to Reflection* (1829), are devoted to an examination of Coleridge; the main topic of the essay, however, is a discussion of "German metaphysics, which seem . . . to be called for by the present state of feeling among literary men in relation to this subject" (p. 129). Henry Pochmann's monumental *German Culture in America: Philosophical and Literary Influences, 1600-1900* (Madison, Wis., 1961) has a concise and very useful discussion of Hedge's role as disseminator of German thought in America (pp. 144-48). Pochmann's book is, of course, invaluable on this subject.

21. Marsh's translation of Johann G. von Herder's *Vom Geist der Ebraischen Poesie, Eine Anleitung fur die Liebhaber derselben, und der*

altesten Geschichte des menschichen Geistes (Dessau, 1782) was first
published by Charles Hodge in the *Biblical Repertory*, 1 (1826), 327-
427, 506-45, and vol. 3, 429-44; and later in two volumes as *The Spirit
of Hebrew Poetry* (Burlington, Vt., 1833). George Ripley published his
review of Marsh's translation in 1833 in the *Christian Examiner* and
eventually developed it into a series of three articles, the final one in
1836 pleading for Calvinists and Unitarians to recognize that Schleiermacher should be studied in order to resolve the controversy between
rationalists and supernaturalists, or common sense logic and German in-
tuitionalists. *See Christian Examiner,* 18-20 (1835-36), 167-221, 172-204,
1-46.

22. Hodge said in his note at the end of Marsh's final installment of
the translation of Herder, "It is hardly necessary to remark, that in many
of the speculations of the *Author,* neither the translator nor editor have
any faith." *Biblical Repertory,* 2 (1836), 545.

23. The Ripley-Norton controversy began in 1836 after Ripley published
an article on Harriet Martineau's *Rationale of Religious Inquiry (Christian
Examiner,* 20 [1836]). Norton, in the *Boston Daily Advertiser,* condemned
Ripley as an infidel. Ripley responded the next day. Then in 1839 Norton
published *A Discourse on the Latest Form of Infidelity* and the debate began in earnest. Clarence Gohdes's *Periodicals of American Transcendentalism* (pp. 59-60) lists the chief documents in the controversy: *A Discourse
on the Latest Form of Infidelity,* by Andrews Norton (Cambridge, 1839);
The Latest Form of Infidelity Examined, a letter to Mr. Andrews Norton
occasioned by his discourse before the Association of the Alumni of the
Cambridge Theological School, on July 19, 1839, by an alumnus of the
school (Ripley) (Boston, 1839); *Remarks on a Pamphlet Entitled "The
Latest Form of Infidelity Examined,"* by Andrews Norton (Cambridge,
1839); *Defense of "The Latest Form of Infidelity Examined,"* on Spinoza,
by George Ripley (Boston, 1840); *A Third Letter to Mr. Andrews Norton,*
on Schleiermacher and De Wette, by George Ripley (Boston, 1840); *A
Letter to Andrews Norton on Miracles as the Foundation of Faith,* by
Richard Hildreth (Boston, 1840); *Two Articles from the Princeton Re-
view, Concerning the Transcendental Philosophy of the Germans and of
Cousin, and Its Influences on Opinion in this Country,* ed. by Andrews
Norton (Cambridge, 1840). The two articles from the *Princeton Review*
were by James W. Alexander, Alexander B. Dod, and Charles Hodge, and
appear in volumes 11 and 12. The final relevant title was *The Previous
Question Between Mr. Andrews Norton and His Alumni Moved and
Handled in a Letter to All Those Gentlemen,* by Levi Blodgett (Theodore
Parker) (Boston, 1840).

24. Herbert W. Schneider, *History of American Philosophy* (New York,
1946), 246. *See also* Richard Peterson, "Scottish Common Sense in America, 1768-1850," (Ph.D. diss., American University, 1963), 49-50.

25. *CAD*, 79-82, James Marsh to Samuel Taylor Coleridge, March 23, 1829. While Marsh seems to have arranged for the readings in the senior year philosophy course at UVM to avoid the Scottish writers, during his years at Hampden-Sydney College in Virginia (1823-26) Stewart's *Philosophy of the Mind* was included in the curriculum after 1823 by an act of the Board of Trustees; cf. Alfred J. Morrison, ed., *The College of Hampden-Sydney Calendar of Board Minutes, 1776-1876* (Richmond, 1912), n. pag.

26. All of the occupants of the Alfred Chair at Harvard were enthusiastic proponents of the Scottish school; *see*, for example, James Walker's annotated abridgment of Reid's *Essays on the Intellectual Powers* (1850); a seven volume edition of Dugald Stewart's works published in 1829; and, in a definitive statement of the Scottish theory of knowledge, Levi Hedge's *Elements of Logick* (Boston, 1816). On the influence of Scottish common sense philosophy in the classroom and beyond see William Charvat, *The Origins of Critical Thought in America* (Philadelphia, 1936), esp. ch. 3. Charvat points out that Hugh Blair's *Lectures on Rhetoric and Belles Lettres*, a textbook, was studied by at least half of the educated English-speaking world in its day, which was a long one (p. 44).

27. Quoted in Spencer, *Quest for Nationality*, 93.

28. Howe, *Unitarian Conscience*, 183-84.

29. Herman Melville, *Moby Dick, or, The Whale*, ed. by Charles Feidelson, Jr. (New York, 1964), 213-15.

30. Ralph Waldo Emerson, *Complete Works* (Boston, 1895), IX, 15.

31. Blair's *Rhetoric* was adopted by Columbia, Pennsylvania, Brown, North Carolina, Middlebury, Williams, Hamilton, and numerous other colleges between 1800 and 1835. Most American rhetoric texts were derived from Kames and Blair, including school texts with question and exercise sections. *See* Charvat, 32; and Charles Fritz, "The Content of the Teaching of Speech in the American College before 1850" (Ph.D. diss., New York University), 64.

32. Mason Wade, ed., *The Journals of Francis Parkman* (New York, 1947), I, 61-73.

33. Charvat, *Origins*, 50-52.

CHAPTER EIGHT

NATURE'S ROMAN SCOURGED

Congregations attending Burchard's revivals and others throughout the country warmly agreed with their revival leaders' con-
demnations of their sinful lives. The colorful language of revivalists painted a picture of their existence which they willing-
ly accepted. While the Marshes could find in Burchard's revivals no sense of inner reflectiveness that led to the spiritual
humility they believed necessary for true conversions, they still
could recognize that the revivalists' audiences, if only temporarily,
were brought to a sense of their own inadequacies and imperfection, their sins. In this the Marshes and other critics of the revivals shared with Burchard's followers a Calvinistic view of their
own lives, of man's existence, as beset with difficulties and enormous trials. When George Perkins Marsh told his father Charles
in Woodstock that the error he found in Burchard's work was
that the revivalist claimed results from purely human means
which, in the Burlington lawyer's eyes, were impossible because
of the very nature of man that Burchard portrayed in his sermons
and exhortations, he was arguing from a shared assumption about
conditions of life and the nature of man that stood equally at the
base of Burchard's own Measures, the criticism of those Measures
by the Marshes, the criticism of the philo*patriotes* by the "wise

ones of Burlington," and indeed David Read's prayer that the
Jacobinism of the present would someday evolve to a "more
elevated stage of human perfectability."

There was an implicit hopefulness in the minds of both sides
of these controversies. As Frederick Hedge pointed out, the message of Coleridge and Kant to Americans gave them a justification for assertions of individuality and equality in the social and
political life of the country. "A nation of men" would come,
Emerson vaguely promised, if we would recognize our true relationship with nature and patiently be ourselves. A similar hopefulness lies at the base of those resolutions proclaiming liberty
for Canadians and Vermonters, in the revivals' promise of a
"heaven on earth," and in James Marsh's goal of an alumni of
educated democrats. The Coleridgean curriculum, both associa-
tionistic and idealistic aesthetics, New Measure revivals, and
the defense of Canadian and Vermont liberties with the sanctions of the Spirit of '76, all promised a regenerated spirit, a
reconstructed social reality, a unity of self and other.

The resolutions passed at the various public meetings held
in support of the *patriotes* and the petition from Burlington to
Governor Jenison, as it was explained by James Marsh to David
Read, equally assumed the need for social and political conditions in which the possibilities for individual liberties would
be assured. The resolutions passed at Saint Albans and other
towns in Vermont repeatedly expressed apprehension and even
fear at the possibility of violence breaking out in Vermont. The
meeting at Saint Albans on December 19, 1837, considered "it
not improbable that acts of violence might be attempted, and
even that a gang of marauders might be gathered together and
led to make some petty invasion into our territory, disturbing
the public peace and committing acts of outrage . . . a state of
suspense and doubt is not to be endured."[1] The petition to the
governor from the twenty-three citizens of Burlington was similarly concerned with the potential for violent disorder in Vermont
during the winter of 1837. "Every right principled man is necessarily a friend of order and of peace," the petition urged. More-

over, if Americans were indeed "right principled," they should
recognize the dangers in the course of philo*patrio*tism: "The
blessings of order and law are certain—the benefits of revolution
are always beforehand doubtful."

While philo- and anti*patriotes* located the source of potential
violence against Americans in different places—the resolutions
generally cited threats from loyalists in Canada; the Burlington
petition feared a war with England—both parties to the debate
over supporting the Canadian exiles felt themselves threatened
from beyond national boundaries. The raid on the *Caroline* and
some loyalist incursions on the Vermont border in search of
patriotes rumored to be hiding south of the line produced a
double-edged fear throughout the state. The philo*patriotes*,
on one hand, called for the formation of Vermont irregular
defense forces; anti*patriotes* reminded supporters of the Canadian view that giving guns to frightened men could lead to even
greater violence in a full-scale war with England. Various fearful expressions of violence disrupting the social and political
order of Vermont differed only in emphasis, though they developed from similar assumptions about the conditions necessary
for society to survive.

The forms in which fear was expressed can be further determined. Anglophobic resolutions produced at the many meetings held across northern and central Vermont frequently invoked the "Spirit of the Green Mountain Boys." The meeting at
Swanton Falls on January 5, 1838, "Resolved, that . . . it is
written in the Green Mountain Code whoso shedeth the blood
of a citizen of the United States, by Green Mountain Boys his
very heart's *blood* shall be shed."[2] The January 2 meeting at
Westford, "Resolved, That we, as Green Mountain Boys, will use
the liberty our forefathers did, to destroy every principle of
Toryism and at the hazard of our lives prevent any intermed-
dling with the rights of our citizens."[3] Within sixty years of
the original Green Mountain Boys' adventures, first against
provincial New York's claims to land in the Hampshire Grants,
later in the Revolutionary War at Ticonderoga and Bennington,
and for fourteen years during and after the Revolution in the

continued conflict with New York State over land jurisdiction
in the western parts of the independent Republic of Vermont,
the citizen-soldiers led by Seth Warner, the Allens, and Remember Baker had been enthroned in the pantheon of Vermont folk
myth. Daniel Pierce Thompson's novel, *The Green Mountain
Boys*, was not published until 1839; but the Montpelier lawyer's
romantic narrative of events in Vermont during an earlier time
of violent conflict with England quickly found an eager audience.

The repeated invocation of the spirit of the Green Mountain
Boys at various meetings became a kind of formula, then, by
which actions in the present were sanctioned through association with supposedly similar actions in the past. Based on a
simplified view of America's revolutionary past and impelled by
present fears, an ideology was being formed by associative recol-
lections of earlier American efforts to establish an independent
nation. The process attempted to bring proven values and attitudes from a mythic past to a developing ideology of democratic assertiveness in the present. Invoking the "Spirit of the
Green Mountain Boys," or the slightly variant invocation of
the "Spirit of '76," both often linked with paraphrases of
Jefferson's Declaration of Independence, contributed to forming an ideology which could fill in by association a frame of
reference for men badly needing such a frame during troublesome, uncertain times.

The impulse that gave expression to the petition from Burlington to Governor Jenison, however, was no less based on a
mythology than the philo*patriotes*' resolutions which invoked
an American revolutionary past. Especially as the meaning of
the petition to the governor was explained to David Read by
James Marsh, it is apparent that the anti*patriotes* opposed
militant support of the Canadian exiles because they viewed
such actions as purely emotional, and thus incomplete, responses
to events which, by virtue of their complexity and larger implications for international relations, especially with England,
demanded a response based on judgments made by men whose
emotions and intellects were organically integrated. The Marshes,
Torrey, Wheeler, the Benedicts, and their circle have been various-

ly called the Vermont or Conservative Transcendentalists.[4] For
Marsh and the Vermont Transcendentalists, the romantic quest
for perfect ideal unity was qualified by a Calvinistic sense of the
reality of imperfection. Their vestigial Calvinism in political
and social matters assessed men as nowhere near a state of personal unity in which the ideals of Reason—complete political
freedom, for instance—might be realized for collective purposes.
A reconstructed social reality was needed, but one which depended
on a regenerated man. The faculty of the University of Vermont
saw its major role as cultivators of that regenerated man. The
other sixteen signers of the petition to Governor Jenison were
all supporters of the university's objectives, either as members of
the board of corporators or as financial contributors to the university's maintenance.

The petitioners were anti*patriotes* and, earlier, anti-Burchard,
then, because they saw no sign of the regenerated man at the
meetings in support of the Canadian exiles or New Measure revivals. Resolutions expressing sympathy for the *patriotes* in the
language of political abstraction, without considering the possibilities of violence or that greedy men could turn such meetings and resolutions into platforms for forwarding selfish plans
to annex Canada with its open lands, rich resources, and markets,
confirmed for the Vermont Transcendentalists Calvin's harsh
estimate of corrupt human nature. Similarly, from the point of
view of Burchard's critics, an act of the Will alone could not
regenerate a fallen mankind. The enormous expenditure of emotional and physical energy by Burchard in his acrobatic exhortations and his anxious congregation's lamentations for their
sins were simply feeble acts of the Will, all lacking, as the faculties
at Middlebury College and the university claimed, the integrating
force of Reason and Understanding working in unison. The only
hope for regeneration was to look inward, and reflect carefully
on the motives and causes for actions. One should know the past,
of course, whether the past of Revolutionary heroism or the
past of one's own sinful life, but not use it simply as an associative sanction for or prohibition against behavior in the present.
The focus of the petitioners' concern was inward and individual;

in Marsh's terms "spiritual." Turn inward and reflect for a moment, they said, and the true meaning of your actions will become apparent.

Philo*patriotes*, on the other hand, in their reliance on an American patriotic mythology as a sanction for their actions, echo the self-conscious invocations of America's past heard through the literature of the "quest for nationality" in the antebellum period. In the language of associationist theory, using material from America's past as Cooper, Simms, or the composers of the philo*patriote* resolution at Westford, Vermont, did, would induce beneficial, supportive emotions. In associationist aesthetics, the emotion of beauty is produced by linking agreeable ideas in the imagination through various objects associated with simple emotions. American literary and art critics especially approved of art works which associated objects of large social and national significance at the expense of subjective concerns. In political and social matters, as in the debate over supporting the Canadian *patriotes*, linking the Green Mountain Boys, Jefferson's declaration of political independence, and names like John Hancock and Sam Adams when they appeared in the resolutions passed at the meetings held to express sympathy with the *patriotes* induced the emotions and feelings of unity with other men from which the strength to face real or imagined danger could grow.

While the quest inward for personal unity was the basis of the petition drawn up by the "wise ones of Burlington," the resolutions of the philo*patriotes* were generally informed by the ideals of a heroic past which would organize social energies into a community of feeling and action. Earlier the anti-Burchardites in 1835 saw the church as the only institution through which the inward quest for personal integration in Christ's saving grace was possible, while New Measure revivals stood as a threat to that institution. Revival participants, on the other hand, were convinced through the emotional conversion experience that they had entered into a community of feeling with other converted Christians. The community of action, as in the Hartford, Connecticut, Free Church, would come through the effects of social organization that membership in the church entailed. The enthusiasm of some Americans for revivals and defending liberty in the 1830s in Canada or the United States, to others appeared to conflict with a need to sustain established social and political institutions and values, just as the quest for personal unity with its emphasis on organizing the energies of the inner self opposed the quest for an organization of the externally directed energies of group relationships in the ideal framework of a heroic past. Yet the central thrust of each quest is similar in its basic conservatism. The general concern of both the petition and the resolutions, of revivals and their critics, that social chaos and even violence threaten American society and Vermont, is fundamentally shared. They differ only in how they develop from this initial emphasis. From this basic concern and similar initial emphasis, which are obvious symptoms of a young society, developing and uncertain, the felt need for either inward perfection or outward protection led to contradictory responses on the two sides of the debate in Vermont over supporting the *patriotes'* cause.

Ultimately, however, both the introspective cultivation of the individual from raw citizen to divinely inspired democrat, as professed by Marsh and other Transcendentalists, and the identification of the individual with the mass at a revival meeting failed to provide the security many Americans sought. Some Vermonters might feel like Ethan Allen *en masse* as they took up arms against a "royal" enemy north of the border; others might feel like Christ as they dashed from the "anxious bench" to the altar with "fire in the soul." But Herman Melville saw that neither way was finally secure. The Transcendental way could lead to solipsistic vortices yawning below the crow's nest. The rampant individualism of Ethan Allen or John Paul Jones, as Melville suggested in *Israel Potter*, could rend the social fabric if left unchecked.[5]

In 1837, Abraham Lincoln already understood the darker side of the democratic soul. Recognizing that democracy's tolerance for pluralized moralities could drive its leaders paradoxically to use brutal force to support such tolerance, Lincoln

pointed to recent riots and called for total respect for law and
order so as to assure against social chaos and despotism.[6] The
grim vision informing Lincoln's speech to the young men of
Springfield would see its fulfillment in the Civil War. And in
1863 after the New York draft riots, Herman Melville, his
own grim vision of democracy's potential when totally committed to self-reliant individualism now vindicated by the war,
commented:

> Wise Draco comes, deep in the midnight roll
> Of black artillery; he comes, though late;
> In code corroborating Calvin's creed
> And cynic tyrannies of honest kings;
> He comes, nor parlies; and the Town, redeemed,
> Gives thanks devout; nor, being thankful, heeds
> The grimy slur on the Republic's faith implied,
> Which holds that man is naturally good,
> And—more—is Nature's Roman, never to be scourged.[7]

The Civil War, then, in its Draconian horrors and Calvinistic
recognition of corruption, struck a balancing note against the
ninety-year-old democratic claims that because Americans are
free they will always and everywhere be socially purposive and
responsible.

In the 1830s in Vermont and the nation, these moments of
social disruption that were sometimes violent and destructive
and at other times simply threatening to reform local social
arrangements and emotions speak out from basic tendencies
and tensions in a democracy. But as expressions of democratic
characteristics, David Grimsted so cogently reminds us, they
sharply trace profound dilemmas in the society.[8] Forceful
repression by the state at such moments can harm groups who
conform to precepts of law. But for the state to look away
could be to collaborate in the destruction of those very values
a democratic state must protect. As Grimsted further remarks,
Americans in the 1830s lived in the "shadow of twin totalitarian-
isms"—total submission to the state's power, on one hand, or

tyranny by groups or individuals because of a weak state.[9] Americans, certainly the Vermonters we have seen here, knew these dangers well as they proceeded through the anxious, democratic 1830s.

NOTES

1. "Great Meeting at St. Albans," *Vermont Mercury*, December 29, 1837. Two thousand "freemen of the County of Franklin" gathered for this meeting.

2. "Meeting of Freemen at Swanton Falls," *Danville North Star*, January 12, 1838.

3. *Burlington Sentinel*, January 11, 1838.

4. Lewis S. Feuer, "James Marsh and the Conservative Transcendentalist Philosophy: A Political Interpretation," *New England Quarterly*, 31 (1958), 3-31.

5. Herman Melville, *Israel Potter* (New York, 1855).

6. Abraham Lincoln, "Address Before the Young Men's Lyceum of Springfield, January 27, 1838," in *Collected Works*, ed. by Roy P. Basler (New Brunswick, 1953), I, 110-12; cited in Grimsted, "Rioting," 396.

7. Herman Melville, " 'The House-Top' / A Night Piece / (July, 1863)," *Selected Poems*, ed. by Hening Cohen (Garden City, N.Y., 1964), 90. For a thorough analysis of Melville's vision as it was influenced by Calvinism, *see* T. Walker Herbert, Jr., *Moby Dick and Calvinism: A World Dismantled* (New Brunswick, 1977).

8. Grimsted, "Rioting," 396.

9. Hugh Davis Graham, "The Paradox of American Violence: a Historical Approach," *Annals of the American Academy of Political and Social Science*, 391 (1970), 75-82; cited in Grimsted, "Rioting," 364.

SOURCES

A NOTE ON SOURCES

A basic assumption of this book—that American history can be fruitfully examined through the study of a region, state, or locality—led our search for records and documents to state and local collections like those found in the Vermont Historical Society, Dartmouth College, and the University of Vermont, as well as such obvious national depositories as the Library of Congress and the Public Archives of Canada. Important manuscript collections have been preserved in the regions of their production, and they reveal both quotidian and exceptional concerns and responses of Americans and Canadians to some of the major moments of life in the 1830s.

Collections we consulted included the James Marsh, the George Perkins Marsh, and the George Wyllys Benedict Collections at the University of Vermont and Dartmouth College; the Kellogg Papers at the Vermont Historical Society; and other general manuscript collections in those depositories.

Files of Vermont's newspapers, of which twenty were published during the 1830s, have been well preserved at the University of Vermont and the state library in Montpelier. They, too, proved extremely useful.

The published literature we cite or refer to as support or suggestion further indicate the range of our debt. We have turned to conventional historical narratives as well as analyses of the 1830s produced by such Canadian scholars as Fernand Ouellet and D. G. Creighton, whose studies of Canadian economic and social history during this period were especially helpful; and such American students of the thirties as David Grimsted and Donald G. Mathews, whose works on rioting and revivals examine important aspects of the American experience in the Age of Jackson.

The local dimensions of American history as seen in our view of the Green Mountain State have been a topic studied in the pages of *Vermont History*, the quarterly journal of the Vermont Historical Society, for many decades and in monographs like David Ludlum's *Social Ferment in Vermont, 1791-1850*. Both of us have served as editors of *Vermont History* and have come thereby to appreciate the value to our own research of the great fund of information contained in that and other similar journals of state and local history.

MANUSCRIPT COLLECTIONS

The George Wyllys Benedict Collection, Bailey-Howe Library, UVM.

The Alexander Catlin Collection, Bailey-Howe Library, UVM.

The Comings Collection, Bailey-Howe Library, UVM. A photocopy collection of UVM-related mss of which the originals are deposited in the library of Oberlin College.

Records of the First Congregational Church of Burlington, Vermont, Bailey-Howe Library, UVM.

Hopkins, John Henry. "Diary of a Journey to England, 1837-38." VHS mss collections, Montpelier, Vermont.

The Kellogg Papers, VHS mss collections, Montpelier, Vermont.

The George Perkins Marsh MSS, Baker Library, Dartmouth College.

The James Marsh Collections, Bailey-Howe Library, UVM. A photocopy and holograph collection of mss gathered from various private and public collections.

PAC, RG4, B37, Vol. I; CO. 42, Vols. 274 to 280; S, Vols.
    391-92, 395.
Minutes of the Rutland County Association of Congregational
    Ministers, VHS mss collections, Montpelier, Vermont.
The Joseph Torrey Collection, Bailey-Howe Library, UVM.

NEWSPAPERS

Baltimore *Republican*, August 20, 1835.
Burlington, Vermont, *Free Press*, December 8, 15, 1837; January
    5, 26, 1838; February 22 and March 2, 1838.
Burlington *Vermont Centinel*, August 5, 10, 12, 1808.
Burlington *Vermont Sentinel*, February 22, 1838.
Danville *Vermont North Star*, January 6, 12, 1838.
Montpelier *Vermont Watchman*, January 9, 1838; February 12,
    1838.
Montreal *Gazette*, March 6, 1838.
Philadelphia *National Gazette*, August 11, 1835.
Swanton *Vermont Patriot*, December 27, 1837.
Woodstock *Vermont Mercury*, December 8, 20, 29, 1837; January 26, 29, 1838; December 8, 1838.

BOOKS

Allen, Ethan. "The Capture of Fort Ticonderoga." From *A Narrative of Col. Ethan Allen's Captivity*. Walpole, N.H.: Thomas and Thomas, 1807.
Anderson, Quentin. *The Imperial Self: An Essay in American Literary and Cultural History*. New York: Knopf, 1971.
Bate, Walter Jackson. *Coleridge*. New York: Macmillan, 1968.
Beardsley, Frank G. *A History of American Revivals*. New York: American Tract Society, 1904.
Bell, Andrew. *Men and Things in America*. 2nd. ed. Southampton: For the Author, 1862.
Bodo, John R. *The Protestant Clergy and Public Issues, 1812-1848*. Princeton: Princeton Univ. Press, 1954.
Buckingham, James Silk. *America, Historical, Statistic, and*

Descriptive. 3 vols. London and Paris: Fisher, Sons and Co., 1841.

Cabot, James Eliot. *A Memoir of Ralph Waldo Emerson.* Boston: Houghton Mifflin, 1887.

Cantril, Hadley. *The Psychology of Social Movements.* New York: Wiley, 1963.

Charvat, William. *The Origins of Critical Thought in America.* Philadelphia: Univ. of Pennsylvania Press, 1936.

Clark, S. D. *Movements of Political Protest in Canada, 1640-1840.* Toronto: Univ. of Toronto Press, 1959.

Cole, Charles C. *The Social Ideas of the Northern Evangelists, 1820-1860.* New York: Columbia Univ. Press, 1954.

Coleridge, Samuel Taylor. *Aids to Reflection, in the formation of a Manly Character, on the Several Grounds of Prudence, Morality, and Religion; illustrated by select passages from our elder divines, especially from Archbishop Leighton.* 1st American ed., from 1st London ed. With an appendix and illustrations from other works of the same author, together with a preliminary essay and additional notes from James Marsh. Burlington, Vt.: Chauncey Goodrich, 1829.

——. *The Friend: A Series of Essays, To Aid in the Formation of Fixed Principles in Politics, Morals, and Religion, with Literary Amusements Interspersed.* 1st American ed. Burlington, Vt.: Chauncey Goodrich, 1831.

The College of Hampden-Sydney Calendar of Board Minutes, 1776-1876. Ed. by Alfred J. Morrison. Richmond, Va.: Hermitage Press, 1912.

Cooper, James Fenimore. *The Pioneers.* New York: C. Wiley, 1823.

Corey, Albert B. *The Crisis of 1830-1842 in Canadian-American Relations.* New Haven: Yale Univ. Press, 1941.

Creighton, Donald Grant. *The Commercial Empire of the St. Lawrence.* Toronto: Ryerson Press, 1937.

Crocker, Henry. *History of the Baptists in Vermont.* Bellows Falls, Vt.: P. H. Gobie Press, 1913.

Cross, Whitney. *The Burnt-Over District: The Social and Intellectual History of Enthusiastic Religion in Western New York, 1825-50.* Ithaca: Cornell Univ. Press, 1950.

Daniels, Bruce C. *The Connecticut Town*. Middletown, Conn.: Wesleyan Univ. Press, 1979.

De Celles, Alfred. *Louis-Joseph Papineau*. Toronto: Morang, 1910.

Dickens, Charles. *American Notes for General Circulation*. Philadelphia: J. B. Lippincott, 1891.

Duffy, John, ed. *Coleridge's American Disciples: Selected Correspondence of James Marsh*. Amherst: Univ. of Massachusetts Press, 1973.

——. *Early Vermont Broadsides*. Hanover, N.H.: University Press of New England, 1975.

Eastman, Charles G., ed. *Sermons, Addresses and Exhortations of Jedidiah Burchard*. Burlington, Vt.: Chauncey Goodrich, 1836.

Ellis, William Arba, ed. *Norwich University/1819-1911/Her History, Her Graduates, Her Roll of Honor*. 3 vols. Montpelier, Vt.: Capitol City Press, 1911.

Emerson, Ralph Waldo. *Complete Works*. Boston: Houghton Mifflin, 1895.

Farr, David, J. S. Moir, and S. R. Mealing. *Two Democracies*. Toronto: Ryerson Press, 1963.

Fauteaux, Aegidius. *Patriotes de 1837-38*. Montreal: Editions des Dix, 1950.

Filteau, Gerard. *Histoire des Patriotes*. 3 vols. Montreal: Editions de A. C.-F., 1938-1942.

Foster, Charles. *An Errand of Mercy: The Evangelical United Front, 1790-1837*. Chapel Hill: Univ. of North Carolina Press, 1960.

Fritz, Charles. *The Content of the Teaching of Speech in the American College before 1850*. Ph.D. dissertation, New York University, 1956.

Garneau, Francis Zavier. *History of Canada*. Montreal: J. Lovell, 1862.

Graham, Hugh Davis, and T. R. Gurr, eds. *Violence in America: A Documentary History*. New York: New American Library, 1970.

Grund, Francis. *The Americans in Their Moral, Social and Political Relations*. Boston, 1837; rpt. New York: Johnson, 1968.

Hamilton, Thomas. *Men and Manners in America*. 2 vols. London: W. Blackwood and Sons, 1833.

Haskins, Nathan. *A History of the State of Vermont, from its Discovery and Settlement to the Close of the Year MDCCCXXX.* Vergennes, Vt.: J. Shedd, 1831.

Hemenway, Abby Maria, ed. *Poets and Poetry of Vermont.* Rutland, Vt.: Goerge A. Tuttle & Co., 1858.

——. *Vermont Historical Gazetteer.* Various places: various publishers, 1868-80.

Herbert, T. Walter, Jr. *Moby-Dick and Calvinism: A World Dismantled.* New Brunswick, N.J.: Rutgers Univ. Press, 1977.

Herder, Johann G. von. *The Spirit of Hebrew Poetry.* Trans. by James Marsh. Burlington, Vt.: E. Smith, 1833.

Holbrook, Stewart. *The Yankee Exodus.* New York: Macmillan, 1950.

Howe, Daniel. *The Unitarian Conscience: Harvard Moral Philosophy, 1805-1861.* Cambridge: Harvard Univ. Press, 1970.

——, ed. *Victorian America.* Philadelphia: Univ. of Pennsylvania Press, 1976.

Journal of the Vermont House of Representatives, 1838. Montpelier: E. P. Smith, 1838.

Kilbourne, William. *The Firebrand: William Lyon Mackenzie and the Rebellion in Upper Canada.* Toronto: Clarke, Irwin, 1956.

Kinchen, Oscar A. *The Rise and Fall of the Patriot Hunters.* New York: Bookman Associates, 1956.

Labaree, Benjamin W. *Patriots and Partisans: The Merchants of Newburyport, 1764-1815.* New York: Norton, 1975.

The Life, Letters, and Journals of George Ticknor. Boston: Houghton Mifflin, 1880.

Lindsay, Julian. *Tradition Looks Forward / The University of Vermont: A History / 1791-1904.* Burlington: Univ. of Vermont, 1954.

Lockridge, Kenneth. *A New England Town the First Hundred Years.* New York: Norton, 1970.

Lowenthal, David. *George Perkins Marsh: Versatile Vermonter.* New York: Columbia Univ. Press, 1958.

Lower, Arthur R. M. *Canadians in the Making.* Toronto: Longmans, Green, 1958.

Lucas, Charles Prestwood, ed. *Lord Durham's Report on the Affairs of British North America.* Oxford: Clarendon Press, 1912.

Ludlum, David. *Social Fermont in Vermont, 1791-1850.* Montpelier: VHS, 1937.

McGrane, Reginald Charles. *The Panic of 1837.* New York: Russell and Russell, 1965.

Manning, Helen Taft. *The Revolt of French Canada, 1800-1835.* New York: St. Martin's Press, 1962.

Marryat, Captain Frederick. *Diary in America.* Ed. by Jules Zanger. Bloomington: Indiana Univ. Press, 1960.

Melville, Herman. *Israel Potter.* New York: Putnam, 1855.

——. *Moby Dick or, The Whale.* Ed. by Charles Feidelson, Jr. New York: Bobbs, Merrill, 1964.

——. " 'The House Top' / A Night Piece / July 1863," *Selected Poems.* Ed. by Hening Cohen. Garden City, N.Y.: Doubleday, 1964.

Memorial Manual of the Fourth Congregational Church, Hartford, Connecticut. Hartford, 1882.

Mencken, H. L. *The American Language.* New York: Knopf, 1937.

Mumly, James H., and Earle G. Shettleworth, Jr. *The Flight of the Grand Eagle: Charles G. Bryant, Maine Architect and Adventurer.* Augusta: Maine Bicentennial Commission, 1977.

Nevins, Allan, ed. *American Social History As Recorded by British Travellers.* New York: Oxford Univ. Press, 1923.

Nichols, John Hastings. *Romanticism in American Theology.* Chicago: Univ. of Chicago Press, 1961.

Noble, William F. *God's Doings in Our Vineyard.* Philadelphia: H. C. Watts and Co., 1882.

Norwich University / 1819-1911 / Her History, Her Graduates, Her Roll of Honor. 3 vols. Ed. by William Arba Ellis. Montpelier, Vt.: Capital City Press, 1911.

Ouellet, Fernand. *Histoire Economique et Sociale du Quebec 1760-1850.* Montreal: Fides, 1966.

Peterson, Richard. "Scottish Common Sense in America, 1768-1850." Ph.D. dissertation, American University, 1963.

Pochmann, Henry. *German Culture in America: Philosophical and Literary Influences, 1600-1900.* Madison: Univ. of Wisconsin Press, 1961.

The Poetical Works of William Wordsworth. Ed. by Ernest de Selincourt and Helen Darbishire. Oxford: Oxford University Press, 1947.

The Remains of the Rev. James Marsh . . . . Ed. by Joseph Torrey. Boston: Crocker and Brewster, 1843.

Report of the State Trials Before a General Court Martial Held at Montreal in 1838-9 Exhibiting a Complete History of the Late Rebellion in Lower Canada. Montreal, 1839.

Schneider, Herbert W. *History of American Philosophy.* New York: Columbia Univ. Press, 1947.

Schull, Joseph. *Rebellion, The Rising in French Canada 1837.* Toronto: Macmillan, 1971.

The Selected Writings of William Lyon Mackenzie, 1824-1837. Ed. by Margaret Fairley. Toronto: Oxford Univ. Press, 1960.

Spencer, Benjamin. *The Quest for Nationality.* Syracuse: Syracuse Univ. Press, 1957.

Stern, M. P., A. J. Vidich, and D. M. White, eds. *Identity and Anxiety.* Glencoe, Ill.: Free Press, 1960.

Stillwell, Louis D. *Migration from Vermont.* Montpelier: VHS, 1948.

Streeter, Russell. *Mirror of Calvinistic, Fanatical Revivals, or Jedidiah Burchard & Co. During a Protracted Meeting of Twenty-Six Days, in Woodstock, Vt. to which is added the "Preamble and Resolution" of the Town Declaring Said Burchard a Nuisance to Society.* Woodstock, Vt.: C. K. Smith and Co., 1835.

Sullivan, Nell Jane Barnett, and David Kendall Martin. *A History of the Town of Chazy, Clinton County, New York.* Burlington, Vt.: George Little Press, 1970.

Swift, Samuel. *History of the Town of Middlebury.* Middlebury, Vt.: A. H. Copeland, 1859.

Thompson, Daniel Pierce. *The Green Mountain Boys.* Montpelier, Vt.: E. P. Walton, 1839.

Thompson, Zadock. *History of Vermont, Natural, Civil, and Statistical.* Burlington, Vt.: Chauncey Goodrich, 1842.

Tocqueville, Alexis de. *Democracy in America.* Ed. by Philip Bradley. New York: Knopf, 1957.

Trollope, Francis. *Domestic Manners of the Americans.* London: Whittaker, Treacher, and Co., 1832.

Tyler, Alice Felt. *Freedom's Ferment: Phases of American Social History from the Colonial Period to the Outbreak of the Civil War.* New York: Octagon Press, 1972.

Tyler, Royall. *The Contrast.* 1787; rpt. New York: AMS Press, 1970.

Van Deusen, Glyndon G. *William Henry Seward.* New York: Oxford Univ. Press, 1967.

Wade, Mason. *The French Canadians, 1760-1945.* New York: Macmillan, 1955.

———, ed. *The Journals of Francis Parkman.* New York: Harpers, 1947.

Walton, E. P., ed. *Walton's Vermont Register and Almanac, 1837.* Montpelier, Vt.: E. P. Walton, 1837.

Weisberger, Bernard. *They Gathered at the River: The Story of the Great Revivalists and Their Impact Upon Religion in America.* Chicago: Univ. of Chicago Press, 1966.

Wilbur, George B., and Warren Muensterberger, eds. *Psychoanalysis and Culture.* New York: International Universities Press, 1951.

ARTICLES AND PAMPHLETS

Adams, Thurston. "Prices Paid by Vermont Farmers for Goods and Services and Received by Them for Farm Products, 1790-1940; Wages of Vermont Farm Labor, 1790-1940." *Vermont Agricultural Experiment Station Bulletin*, no. 507 (February 1944).

Bassett, T. D. Seymour. "Irish Immigration to Vermont Before the Famine." *Chittenden County Historical Society Bulletin*, no. 4 (March 1966).

Brewster, H. Pomeroy. "The Magic of a Voice." *Rochester Historical Society Publications Fund Series*, 4 (1925), 273-90.

Caron, Abbé Ivanhöe. "Une Société Secrète dans le Bas-Canada en 1838: L'Association des Frères Chasseurs." *Transactions of the Royal Society of Canada.* 3rd Series, 20 (1926), 17-34.

Channing, William Ellery. "The Influence of America on the Mind." *Christian Examiner,* 36 (1830), 262-94.

Craig, G. M. "The American Impact on the Upper Canadian Reform Movement before 1837." *Canadian Historical Review,* 29 (December 1948), 333-52.

Creighton, Donald Grant. "The Economic Background of the Rebellions of Eighteen Thirty-Seven." *Canadian Journal of Economics and Political Science,* 3 (August 1937).

———. "The Struggle for Financial Control in Lower Canada, 1818-1831." *Canadian Historical Review,* 12 (March 1931).

Feuer, Lewis S. "James Marsh and the Conservative Transcendentalist Philosophy: A Political Interpretation." *New England Quarterly,* 31 (1958), 3-31.

Graffagnino, J. Kevin, "The Vermont 'Story': Continuity and Change in Vermont Historiography." *Vermont History,* 46 (Spring 1978), 77-99.

———. "Zadock Thompson and the Story of Vermont." *Vermont History,* 47 (1979), 237-57.

Goubert, Pierre. "Local History." *Daedalus,* 100 (Winter 1971), 113-27.

Grimsted, David. "Rioting in Its Jacksonian Setting." *American Historical Review,* 77 (1972), 364.

Hedge, Frederick Henry. "Coleridge's Literary Character." *Christian Examiner,* 14 (1833), 108-29.

"Journal of Alonzo Jackman's Excursion to Quebec, 1838." Ed. by Gary T. Lord. *Vermont History,* 46 (1978), 244-59.

Jones, R. L. "French Canadian Agriculture in the St. Lawrence Valley, 1815-1837." *Canadian Historical Association Annual Report,* 1962, 17-23.

Keating, Peter. "Victorian Lives." *Times Literary Supplement,* December 7, 1979, 90.

Link, Eugene P. "Vermont Physicians and the Canadian Rebellion of 1837." *Vermont History,* 37 (1969), 178-79.

McKelvey, Blake. "The Irish in Rochester: An Historical Record." *Rochester History,* 19 (October 1956), 4-5.

Maier, Pauline. "Popular Uprisings and Civil Authority in Eighteenth-Century America." *William and Mary Quarterly*, 27 (1970), 3-35.

Mathews, Donald G. "The Second Great Awakening as an Organizing Process, 1780-1830." *American Quarterly*, 21 (1969), 22-43.

Muller, H. Nicholas. "Smuggling into Canada: How the Champlain Valley Defied Jefferson's Embargo." *Vermont History*, 38 (1970), 5-21.

Ouellet, Fernand. "Papineau dans la Revolution de 1837-1838." *Canadian Historical Association Annual Report*, 1958, 13-34.

Overman, W. C., ed. "A Sidelight on the Hunter's Lodges of 1838." *Canadian Historical Review*, 19 (1938), 168-72.

Parker, W. H. "A New Look at Unrest in Lower Canada in the 1830s." *Canadian Historical Review*, 40 (September 1959).

Rezneck, Samuel. "The Social History of the American Depression, 1837-1843." *American Historical Review*, 60 (1935), 662-87.

Shortridge, W. P. "The Canadian-American Frontier During the Rebellion of 1837." *Canadian Historical Review*, 7 (1926), 13-26.

Stone, Lawrence. "English and United States Local History." *Daedulus*, 100 (Winter 1971), 128-32.

Tiffany, Orvis E. "The Relations of the United States to the Canadian Rebellion." *Publications of the Buffalo Historical Society*, 8 (1905), 1-147.

Wade, Mason. "The French Parish and *Survivance* in Nineteenth-Century New England." *Catholic Historical Review*, 36 (1950), 163-89.

Wilson, Harold F. "Population Trends in North-Western New England, 1790-1930." *New England Quarterly*, 7 (1934), 276-77.

Wood, Gordon. "A Note on Mobs in the American Revolution." *William and Mary Quarterly*, 23 (1966), 635-42.

INDEX

Adams, Henry, 70
Aids to Reflection (Coleridge), 96, 107, 112, 114, 133. *See also* Coleridge, Samuel Taylor
Alison, Archibald, 133-37
Allen, Ethan, 9; attacks aristocracy, 104, impact on Vermont image, 121-24, 149. *See also* Allen family
Allen, Ira, 121. *See also* Allen family
Allen family, 9, 146. *See also* Allen, Ethan; Allen, Ira
American Scholar, The (Emerson), 127
"Ancient and Modern Poetry" (James Marsh), 107-8
Anti-Mason Party, 22, 109
Antiquitates Americanae, 117
Aroostock War, 50
associationism, 133-36. *See also* Alison, Archibald; Thompson, Daniel Pierce
Atlantic Magazine, 136
Auburn Theological Seminary, 34

Bailey, Benjamin R., 107-8
Baker, Remember, 146
Baldwin, Jonathan, 36
Bancroft, George, 130
Barlow, Isaac, 33
Bate, Walter Jackson, 96
Bates, John, 33
Bates, Joshua, 27, 29
Bell, Andrew, 60
Benedict, Abner, 34
Benedict, Farrand, 34, 87
Benedict, George Wyllys, 28, 87
Biblical Repertory, 111, 131-33
Blackwood's Magazine, 137
Bouchette, Robert, 92
Brainerd, David, 33
Brown, Thomas Storrow, 52, 58, 93; described by Marryat, 17; in Middlebury, 62, 66-67
Brownson, Orestes, 129
Bryant, William Cullen, 129
Buchanan, James, 71
Buell, Harriet, 108
Buell, Ozias, 108
Bunyan, John, 33

Burchard, Jedidiah, 8, 11, 40n; branded public nuisance, 26; converted by Finney, 24; Bishop Hopkins's opposition to, 37-38; left little ground for neutrality, 27-28; James Marsh's opposition to, 33-35, 37, 41n, 113-14, 143; and New Measure system in Vermont, 6-7, 24-25; opposed by Congregational leaders, 26-33; opposed by professional class, 26-27; provides contrast between ideational rhetoric and reality, 125; response to, illustrates tensions in democratic society, 13; response to critics, 30-31; returns to New York, 37; Vermont Baptists and, 35-37. *See also* Marsh, James; New Measure System; revivalism; Vermont: Baptists in; Vermont: Congregational church in

Burlington, Vt., 6, 22; Baptists in, 36; debt imprisonment in, 110; described, 39n, 106-7; during Canadian Rebellion, 43, 65; revivalism in, 24-25, 27-29

Burlington Free Press, 52, 68-69, 71

Burlington *Northern Sentinel*, 108

Canadian Patriot, 67

Canadian Rebellion of 1837-1838: American reaction to, 10-11, 46-47, 50-51, 60-61; and American Revolution, 46, 59, 61, 66-67, 92; as seen by Canadian historians, 46-47, 53n; begins, 44; collapses, 60, 96; Vermont reaction to, 6-7, 11, 13, 17, 22, 44-46. *See also* French-Canadians; Jenison, Silas; *Les Frères Chasseurs*; Marsh, James; *patriotes*; Read,

David; United States; Vermont; Vermont, University of

Carlyle, Thomas, 132-33

Caroline, 94, 99, 145

Catlin, Alec: and Gov. Jenison, 70, 117; lends money to *patriotes*, 63; watches for spy, 43-45

Catlin, Guy, 43, 44, 70

Catlin, Henry, 44, 51

Catlin family, 43-46, 49-50, 52. *See also* Catlin, Alec; Catlin, Guy; Catlin, Henry

Choate, Rufus, 111

Christian Spectator, 107

Colborn, Sir John, 69

Coleridge, Samuel Taylor: contrasted with Rousseau, 96-97; contribution to American ideology, 132, 134; influence on James Marsh, 88, 111, 112, 114, 131; philosophy applied to University of Vermont curriculum, 98-99; political themes, 95-98; spiritual philosophy, 33. *See also Aids to Reflection*; *Friend, A Series of Essays..., The*; Marsh, James

Compendious Grammar of Old Northern or Icelandic Language (G. P. Marsh), 112

"Composed on Reading an Account of Misdoings in Parts of America" (Wordsworth), 50

Contrast, The (Tyler), 4

Cooper, James Fenimore, 5, 121, 148; calls for American self-assertion, 128-29

Coté, Cyrile, 52, 58, 62, 72n

Dabney, Richard, 134

Dana, Richard Henry, Jr., 110

Danville (Vt.) *North Star*, 67

Dartmouth College, 104, 133-34

Davidson, Reverend, 34-35
de Tocqueville, Alexis, 6, 47
Dewey, John, 114
Dobsworth, Chancellor, 61
Downing, Jack, 130
Du Contrat Social (Rousseau), 96
Dumez, Eugene, 5
Durham, Lord, 73n, 116, 119

Eastman, Charles G.: and Burchard, 28-29; on Vermont history, 8-9
Eaton, Horace, 69
Edwards, Jonathan, 33
Elements of Criticism (Kames), 134
Emerson, Ralph Waldo, 5; and search for American identity, 14n, 127, 144; pantheism, 135
Everett, Edward, 106, 112, 130

Ferris, F. S., 69
Finney, Charles Grandison, 24, 34, 41n
Fisk, James, 69
Foster, Timothy, 70
Free Church of Hartford (Conn.), 31-32
French-Canadians: and British, 58; discussed by Alonzo Jackman, 117; discussed by George Marsh, 113; discussed by James Marsh, 89, 113; try to resist English-speaking society, 57-58; in Vermont, 51, 54n
Friend, The (newspaper), 95
Friend: A Series of Essays, to Aid in the Formation of Fixed Principles in Politics, Morals and Religion, The (Coleridge), 88, 95-97, 107. *See also* Coleridge, Samuel Taylor
Fuller, Austin, 69

Gagnon, Julius, 92
Garrison, William Lloyd, 22
Gates, Judge, 63
Goodrich, Chauncey, 88; and Burchard, 28-29
Gosford, Lord, 44-45
Goths in New England, The (G. P. Marsh), 113
Goubert, Pierre, 8
Green Mountain Boys: as portrayed by Daniel Thompson, 122-25; spirit of, invoked during Canadian Rebellion, 145-46, 148
Green Mountain Boys, The (Thompson), 125, 146; creates image of Vermonters, 121; portrayal of Ethan Allen, 122-24. *See also* Green Mountain Boys; Thompson, Daniel Pierce
Grimsted, David, 150
Grund, Francis, 5

Hagner, Peter, 119
Hall, Hiland, 121
Hamilton, Thomas, 20
Hartley, David, 133
Hedge, Frederick Henry, 131-32, 144
Herder, Johann: influence on George Ticknor, 130; translated by James Marsh, 111, 132
Hickok, Samuel, 29
Higginson, T. W., 112
Hill, Isaac, 95
Hillhouse, James, 129
Hodge, Charles, 133
Hopkins, Heman, 69
Hopkins, Bishop John Henry: opposes Burchard, 27; opposes revivalism and philo*patriote* sentiment, 37-38
Hume, David, 133
Hunters' Lodges. *See Les Frères Chasseurs*

Idealism, influence of German, on
    U.S. thought, 130-34
Ingersoll, Charles, 128

Jackman, Alonzo, 114, 122;
    comments on British rule in
    Canada, 117-18; and Norwich
    University's philo*patriote*
    feeling, 118-19; travels in
    Canada, 115-16
Jenison, Silas, 103; elected gover-
    nor, 109, 124; meets with
    Alonzo Jackman, 116, 118-19;
    neutrality proclamation, 71-72;
    petitioned to proclaim neutrali-
    ty, 50, 87-88, 91, 144, 146-47;
    proclamation diminishes *patriote*
    support, 94; rebuked by
    philo*patriotes*, 92; requests
    return of cannon, 70, 117; tours
    border, 64

Kames, Lord, 133
Kant, Immanuel, influence on
    American thought, 131-32, 144
Kasson, Charles B., 70
Kellogg, Daniel, 63-64
Kent, Edward, 70

Lane, Heyman, 43-46
"Leatherstocking Tales"
    (Cooper), 129
Les Frères Chasseurs, 45, 49, 62;
    in Vermont, 50. *See also*
    Patriotes
Lincoln, Abraham, 149-50
Local history, 8-13; importance to
    national history, 11-12
Lord, Nathan, 32, 37
Lowenthal, David, 107-8, 111,
    113-14
Ludlum, David, 48
Lyrical Ballads (Wordsworth), 136

MacKenzie, William Lyon, 49-50,
    130
McNab, Allan, 94
Man and Nature (G. P. Marsh),
    111
Marcy, William L., 49, 61
Marryat, Frederick, 17; impres-
    sions of Americans, 18, 60, 72;
    impressions of Canadian
    Rebellion, 17
Marsh, Charles (father of G. P.
    Marsh), 104, 143
Marsh, Charles (son of G. P.
    Marsh), 108
Marsh, Daniel, 104
Marsh, George Perkins, 98, 103;
    biographical sketch, 103-14;
    business interests, 108; helps
    elect Jenison, 124; language
    studies, 110-13; nativist
    snobbery, 113; opposes
    Burchard and philo*patriotes*,
    114, 143; petitions for Vermont
    neutrality, 87-88; political
    career, 109-10; supports Andrew
    Jackson, 108
Marsh, James, 103, 115; anti-
    Burchard stand, 28, 33, 143;
    attacked for anti-Burchard
    stand, 27, 29; becomes president
    of the University of Vermont,
    106; biographical sketch of,
    104-14; correspondence with
    David Read on Canadian
    Rebellion, 48, 88-100, 144-45;
    death of, 100; education of,
    105-6; fears Burchard's effect
    on Congregational church, 32,
    34-35, 114; influenced by
    German idealism, 113, 132-33;
    introduces Coleridge's
    philosophy to University of
    Vermont, 95, 131, 139n; nativist
    thought of, 90; opposes philo-

patriotes, 45-46, 65, 88-100, 144-49; petitions for Vermont neutrality, 87, 91, 144-49; sees parallels between Burchardism and philo*patriotes*, 37-88; spokesman for Coleridge's political philosophy, 88, 95, 98; spokesman for Coleridge's spiritual philosophy, 33; theoretical and philosophical justification for opposing philo-*patriotes*, 94-98

Marsh, Joseph, 87, 104

Marsh, Orin, 120

Marshall, John, 104

Mathews, Donald, 20

Melville, Herman: views on American individualism, 149-50; warns of dangerous tendencies of German idealism, 134-35

Middlebury, Vt., 24-27; meeting in support of Canadian rebellion, 65-66; *patriote* leaders meet in, 62; supplies cannon to *patriotes*, 63

Middlebury College, 147; faculty criticizes Burchardism, 27

Miller, Jonathan Peckham, 120-21; actively supports *patriotes*, 121

Miller, William, 23

Mirror of Calvinistic, Fanatical Revivals (Streeter), 28

Mitchell, Edward, 36

Montpelier, Vt., 63-64

Montreal Herald, 68, 93

More, Henry, 33, 111

Myrick, Cyrus, 119-20

Neal, John, 129

Nelson, Robert, 58, 65, 70, 72n, 116; becomes *patriote* leader, 62, 66; leads invasions, 62-63, 99; refuses compromise, 64

Nelson, Wolfred, 58

Nettleton, Asahel, 31

Nevins, John W., 95

New Hampshire Patriot, 95

New Measure System: in Hartford, Vt., 31; reaction to, reveals movement of groups within society, 103; threat to Congregationalism, 29, 32-33, 114, 148; in Vermont, 25-27. *See also* Burchard, Jedidiah; Marsh, James; revivalism; Vermont

North American Review, 105-6

Norton, Andrews, 133

Norwich University, 114-16, 124; connection with *patriotes*, 118-20

Noyes, John Humphrey, 23

Observations of Man (Hartley), 133

O'Callaghan, E. B., 58, 62, 72n

Omer (Burlington blacksmith) 43-44, 51

Owens, Robert, 38

Palmer, William, 109, 124

Papineau, Louis-Joseph, 52, 58, 66; inspired by Jacksonian Democracy, 130; inspires *patriote* insurrection, 44; loses leadership of *patriotes*, 62; offered services of Gens. Scott and Wool, 61

Papineau, Louis-Joseph (grandson), 100

Parkman, Francis, 136

Partridge, Alden, 118, 120; educational theory, 115; hires James Marsh, 105. *See also* Norwich University

patriotes, 6, 22; adopt rhetoric of American Revolution, 59;

assemble arms, 62-63; collapse
of rebellion, 61; defeated by
British, 58-60; expect help from
France and Russia, 70;
filibusters into Canada, 62;
leaders flee to U.S. and
Vermont, 58-60, 62-63;
overestimate American support,
64; rout British, 58. *See also*
Brown, Thomas Storrow;
Canadian Rebellion of
1837-1838; Catlin, Alec; French-
Canadians; Jenison, Silas;
Nelson, Robert; Papineau,
Louis-Joseph; United States;
Vermont
Perkins, Captain, 70
Perrault, Louis, 66
Philadelphia National Gazette, 4
Pilgrim's Progress (Bunyan), 33
Pitkin, Caroline, 100

Quebec *Mercury*, 69

Rafn, Carl Christian, 111, 112
Rask, Rasmus Christian, 112
Read, David, 46, 113; corre-
spondence with James Marsh,
45, 48, 88-89, 131, 144, 146;
defense of philo*patriotes*, 88-92,
94-99. *See also* Marsh, James
Reid, Thomas, 133
revivalism: as remedial actions to
allay strains of uncertainty, 23;
as social organizing force, 20;
Hamilton's observations on, 20;
Mrs. Trollope's observations on,
18-19
Rhetoric (Hugh Blair), 134
Rice, John Holt, 106
Ridgely, Samuel, 119
Ripley, George, 111, 132
Rochester, N.Y., revivalism in,
34-35

Rousseau, Jean Jacques, 96-97
Russell, Lord John, 58
Rutland Association of Congregational Ministers: criticized, 27;
oppose Burchard, 26, 30, 32

Saint Albans, Vt., 18, 63-65; and
Canadian Rebellion, 65-66,
68-69, 88, 91-92; resolutions to
protect *patriotes*, 65-66, 92-93,
144
Saint Charles (Canada), 58-60
Saint Denis (Canada), 58-60, 74n
Saint Eustache (Canada), 58, 60
Sawyer, Joseph, 35
Schneider, Herbert W., 133
Scott, Walter, 129
Scott, Gen. Winfred, 50, 61, 99
Scottish Common Sense philos-
ophy, 130, 133-37; 141n
Second Great Awakening, 18, 20,
104. *See also* Burchard, Jedidiah;
revivalism
*Select Practical Theology of the
Seventeenth Century* (James
Marsh), 111
Sessions, Gideon, 124
Seward, William H., 49
Shurtleff, Roswell, 104-5
Silly (Cilly), J. B., 69
Simms, William Gilmore, 121,
134, 148
Smith, Joseph, 23
Sparks, Jared, 131
Spencer, Benjamin, 127
Spirit of Hebrew Poetry (Herder),
108, 111, 130, 132
Spy, The (Cooper), 129
Stacy, Henry, 52, 68, 70, 92
Stevens, Henry, Sr., 121
Stonehaus, M., 69
Streeter, Russell, 28
Swanton, Vt., 62-63, 65, 69-70, 92
Swedenborgianism, 23, 32

Tarbell, Jonathan, 119
Tenny, B. J., 28-29
Thompson, Daniel Pierce, 125;
   employs associationist aesthetics
   in novel, 121; found ready
   audience, 122, 146. *See also*
   associationism
Thompson, Mrs., 34-35
Ticknor, George, 105-6; influenced
   by German idealism, 130-31
Torrey, Joseph, 31, 87, 110
Torrey, Mrs. Joseph, 29
Trollope, Francis (Mrs. Anthony),
   18-20
Truair, John, 32
Tyler, Alice Felt, 47
Tyler, Royall, 3-4

United States: arsenals raided by
   patriotes, 62-64; and collapse of
   Canadian Rebellion, 60; debate
   over meaning of American
   Revolution, 48, 59;
   individualism, 4-6; influence of
   German idealism on, 130-37;
   influence of Scottish philosophy
   on, 130, 134-36; mass
   movements in, 3-5, 8;
   observations on, by foreigners,
   18-20; possibility of rupture
   with Britain, 71; quest for
   national identity, 47-48, 127-29,
   149-50; response to Canadian
   Rebellion, 46-48, 50-51, 87;
   revivals in, 4, 18, 20. *See also*
   Canadian Rebellion of
   1837-1838; *patriotes*; revivalism

Van Buren, Martin, 49-50, 63,
   71-72, 119
Van Ness, Cornelius, 108
Van Rensselaer, Rensselaer, 49, 51
Vermont: anti-Jackson feeling in,

95, 130; antipathy to British, 59;
   background of philo*patriotes* in,
   69; Baptists in, 35-37;
   Congregational church in,
   24-26, 29-32, 34, 36; extraordinary interest in Canadian
   Rebellion, 72; fertile ground for
   social ferment, 22-23; formation
   of *Les Frères Chasseurs* in, 49;
   French-Canadian in, 51; interest
   of, in Canadian Rebellion flags,
   72, 94; mass movements in, 6;
   neutrality of during Rebellion,
   50, 71-72, 87-88, 91, 144,
   146-47; New Measure revivals
   in, 6, 23-24, 27, 34, 37, 103;
   opposes British rule in Canada,
   67-68; opposition to *patriotes*,
   87; panic of 1837 in, 11, 22, 47,
   53n; *patriote* meeting in, 62;
   press and Rebellion, 60; realism
   vs. rhetoric in, 125; resents
   Canadian crackdown on
   smuggling, 68-69; response to
   Canadian Rebellion, 7, 22,
   44-46, 51, 57, 61, 64-65, 144-45;
   response to Rebellion tied to
   revivalism, 37; support for
   patriotes, 6, 37-38, 47-49, 60-61,
   64-65; vast changes in, during
   1830s, 20-21; viewed Rebellion
   as re-enactment of American
   Revolution, 59-60, 66-67;
   weakness of, historiography, 9.
   See also Burchard, Jedidiah;
   Canadian Rebellion of
   1837-1838; Jenison, Silas;
   Marsh, James; Vermont,
   University of
Vermont, University of: faculty
   of, criticized by Burchard, 30;
   faculty of, criticizes Burchard,

27-29, 32; faculty of, redesigns
curriculum according to
Coleridgean distinctions, 98-99;
faculty of, response to Canadian
Rebellion, 7; faculty of, and
Scottish philosophy, 134; faculty
of, views itself as cultivators of
common man, 147; students of,
converted by Burchard, 7. *See
also* Burchard, Jedidiah;
Canadian Rebellion of
1837-1838; Marsh, James;
patriotes; Vermont
Vermont Argus and Free Press, 66
Vermont Chronicle, 87
Vermont Historical Society, 121,
124
Vermont Mercury, 59
Vermont Patriot, 59
Vermont Temperance Society, 22
Vermont Transcendentalism, 147

Vindicator, 66, 67
Vom Geist der Ebraschen Poesie
(Herder), 132

Warner, Seth, 146
War of 1812, 21, 23, 52, 59, 61,
72, 87, 127-128
Webster, Daniel, 104
Webster, J. S., 69
Weeks, Philo, 68
Wheeler, John, 27, 87, 110
Wheelock, Eleazer, 104
Wheelock, John, 104-5
Wheelock, Laura (Mrs. James
Marsh), 108
Wheelock, Lucia (Mrs. James
Marsh), 104-8
Wirt, William, 22
Wool, Gen. John Ellis, 61, 63-64,
71, 124
Wordsworth, William, 50, 52,
136-37

About the Authors

John J. Duffy is Professor of English and Humanities at Johnson State College in Johnson, Vermont. His earlier works include *Coleridge's American Disciples* and *Early Vermont Broadsides*.

H. Nicholas Muller, III, President of Colby-Sawyer College in New London, New Hampshire, Vice-President of the Vermont Historical Society, and editor of the journal *Vermont History*, formerly served as Professor of History at the University of Vermont.

Recent titles in
Contributions in American Studies
Series Editor: Robert H. Walker

The Essays of Mark Van Doren
William Claire, editor

Touching Base: Professional Baseball and American
Culture in the Progressive Era
Steven A. Riess

Late Harvest: Essays and Addresses in American
Literature and Culture
Robert E. Spiller

Steppin' Out: New York Nightlife and the Transformation
of American Culture, 1890-1930
Lewis A. Erenberg

For Better or Worse: The American Influence in the World
Allen F. Davis, editor

The Silver Bullet: The Martini in American Civilization
Lowell Edmunds

Boosters and Businessmen: Popular Economic Thought
and Urban Growth in the Antebellum Middle West
Carl Abbott

Democratic Dictatorship: The Emergent Constitution
of Control
Arthur Selwyn Miller

The Oriental Religions and American Thought:
Nineteenth-Century Explorations
Carl T. Jackson

Contemporaries: Portraits in the Progressive Era
by David Graham Phillips
Louis Filler, editor

Abortion, Politics, and the Courts: *Roe v. Wade*
and Its Aftermath
Eva R. Rubin